Generis
PUBLISHING

AF609604

Enterprise-Wide Data Management

Model for Effective Data Governance Framework in Large Organizations

Chadwick Thompson Okoye

Title: **Enterprise-Wide Data Management**

Model for Effective Data Governance Framework in Large Organizations

ISBN: 979-8-89248-949-2

Author: Chadwick Thompson Okoye

Cover image: www.pixabay.com

Publisher: Generis Publishing
Online orders: www.generis-publishing.com
Contact email: info@generis-publishing.com

Dedication

This book is dedicated to all data governance managers in large organizations who struggle to implement data governance framework within their organizations. Valuable insights are available for improved strategy.

Acknowledgements

I have heard enormous support throughout my doctoral research journey which made it possible for me to achieve this great success. It will not be possible for me to mention everyone who in one way or the other supported me through this journey. I am very grateful to all who have supported me in achieving this great feat.

I am most grateful to God Almighty who has kept me alive and has given me protection and good health. I would also like to express my profound gratitude to my supervisor and dissertation chair of my doctoral research, Professor Andrea Ivanisevic for the continuous support, advice, guidance, critics as well as encouragement provided to me throughout my doctoral research. I say thank you so much, it would have been mission impossible without your support.

I would also extend my gratitude to the staff and management of SSBM for given me the opportunity for this doctoral research in such a reputable institution including all support thereof, all the doctoral students and colleagues for their various contribution throughout my doctoral journey.

Also, I will not forget all the support from my immediate family, particularly my lovely wife Mrs Vivian Okoye, my children, Chiekezie Okoye, Chimazu Okoye and Adaolisa Okoye for being there for me throughout the challenging time of my doctoral research. To those who responded to my questionnaires, I say thank you very much, without you, this wouldn't have been successful.

ABSTRACT

Large organizations generate and process vast amounts of data, making effective data governance frameworks essential for maintaining data quality, security, and compliance. However, implementing governance structures presents challenges, including organizational resistance, lack of expertise, and integration complexities. This dissertation investigates the measurable impact of data governance frameworks on data quality and business outcomes, the key success factors for effective implementation, and the influence of stakeholder perceptions on adoption and success.

The study employs a quantitative research approach, utilizing survey data from 255 professionals across industries such as finance, healthcare, and technology. The analysis applies regression models, correlation analysis, and factor analysis to examine governance effectiveness. Findings indicate a strong positive correlation between governance implementation and data accuracy, consistency, and regulatory compliance. Organizations with well-structured governance models experience enhanced business efficiency, strategic alignment, and improved decision-making capabilities.

Key success factors identified for governance effectiveness include senior management support, role clarity, interdepartmental collaboration, continuous training, and resource availability. Despite these benefits, resistance to change and governance complexity remain significant barriers. Stakeholder perceptions strongly influence adoption, with most professionals recognizing the advantages of governance frameworks but citing complexity and resource constraints as limiting factors.

The research underscores the need for business-aligned, adaptable governance strategies that integrate emerging technologies like AI and automation to streamline processes and enhance compliance. Organizations should focus on fostering a data-driven culture and implementing structured change management initiatives to overcome resistance and optimize governance adoption.

This study contributes empirical insights into enterprise data governance, offering recommendations for improving governance models, refining regulatory compliance strategies, and leveraging technological advancements. Future research should explore longitudinal studies on governance impact, industry-specific governance applications, and AI-driven automation in governance practices.

Data governance frameworks play a critical role in ensuring data integrity, optimizing decision-making, and driving business performance. By addressing implementation challenges and aligning governance with organizational objectives, businesses can enhance operational efficiency, regulatory compliance, and long-term competitiveness in the evolving digital landscape.

Contents

CHAPTER I: Introduction **15**
1.1 Introduction 15
1.2 Evolution and Importance of Enterprise Data Management 16
1.3 Key Drivers and Challenges in Data Governance 20
1.4 Industry-Specific Considerations and Regulatory Landscape 26
1.5 The Role of Technology and Stakeholders in Data Governance 29
1.6 Ethical, Social, and Security Implications of Data Governance 30
1.7 Need for a Conceptual Model for Effective Data Governance 30
1.8 Research Problem 31
1.9 Purpose of Research 32
1.10 Significance of the Study 32
1.11 Research Purpose and Questions 33
CHAPTER II: Review of literature **35**
2.1 Introduction 35
2.2 EDM Impact on BI & Decision-Making and Challenges in EDM Implementation 36
2.3 Challenges in EDM Implementation 36
2.4 Data Architecture & EDM Relationship and Critical Success Factors 37
2.5 Barriers to Effective Data Governance and Implications of Poor Data Governance 38
2.6 Cloud Computing & Data Governance in EDM and Role of Automation in Compliance & Data Integrity 39
2.7 Data Governance Models and Emerging Trends & Best Practices 41
2.8 Future Regulatory Impact on EDM & Data Governance and Business Value & Competitive Advantage of Data Governance 42
2.9 Data Governance Models & Cyber-security 43
2.10 Literature Gaps 44
2.11 Summary 45
CHAPTER III: Methodology **47**
3.1 Overview of the Research Problem 47
3.2 Operationalization of Theoretical Constructs 47
3.3 Research Purpose and Questions 48
3.4 Research Design 49
3.5 Impact of Data Governance on Data Quality & Business Outcomes. 50
3.6 Key Success Factors for Data Governance Implementation 50

3.7 Stakeholder Perceptions on Data Governance 51
3.8 Population and Sample 52
3.9 Participant Selection 53
3.10 Instrumentation 53
3.11 Data Collection Procedures 54
3.12 Data Analysis 55
3.13 Research Design Limitations 56
3.14 Conclusion 57
CHAPTER IV: Results 59
4.1 Introduction 59
4.2 Demographic Information 60
4.3 Impact of Data Governance on Data Quality & Business Outcome .. 67
4.4 Key Success Factors for Data Governance Implementation 90
4.5 Stakeholder Perceptions on Data Governance 107
4.6 Summary of Findings 126
4.7 Conclusion 127
CHAPTER V: Discussion 129
5.1 Discussion of Impact of Data Governance on Data Quality & Business Outcomes 129
5.2 Discussion of Key Success Factors for Data Governance Implementation 130
5.3 Discussion Of Stakeholder Perceptions on Data Governance 132
5.4 Answer's to Research Questions 134
CHAPTER VI: Summary, implications and recommendations 141
6.1 Summary 141
6.2 Implications 142
6.3 Recommendations for Future Research 144
6.4 Conclusion 146
APPENDIX A - Qustionnaire 149
APPENDIX B - Informed consent 153
REFERENCES 155

LIST OF FIGURES

Figure 1. Age Distribution 60
Figure 2. Gender Distribution 61
Figure 3. Position Distribution 62
Figure 4. Industry Sector Distribution 63
Figure 5. Experience Distribution 65
Figure 6. Data Quality Improvement Responses 67
Figure 7. Business Outcomes Improvement Responses 68
Figure 8. Decision Making Enhancement Responses 69
Figure 9. Quality Improvement Post-Governance Responses 70
Figure 10. Data Management & Strategy Alignment Responses 71
Figure 11. Business Process Improvement Responses 72
Figure 12. Correlation Heatmap (Objective 1) 83
Figure 13. Importance of Senior Management Support Responses 90
Figure 14. Role Clarity in Data Governance Responses 91
Figure 15. Training and Awareness Responses 92
Figure 16. Resource Availability Responses 93
Figure 17. Importance of Inter-departmental Communication Responses .. 94
Figure 18. Factor Analysis (Objective 2) 95
Figure 19. Elbow Method Cluster Analysis (Objective 2) 98
Figure 20. Cluster Analysis (Objective 2) 98
Figure 21. Stakeholder Data Governance Perception Responses 107
Figure 22. Challenges due to Resistance to Change Responses 108
Figure 23. Barriers of Resources or Expertise Responses 109
Figure 24. Perceived Benefits vs Challenges Responses 110
Figure 25. Complexity as a Barrier Responses 111
Figure 26. Likert Scale Analysis (Objective 3) 121

CHAPTER I:
INTRODUCTION

1.1 Introduction

In today's data-driven world, organizations generate and manage vast amounts of data that serve as the foundation for decision-making, operational efficiency, and competitive advantage. As enterprises expand, their data ecosystems become increasingly complex, making it essential to establish structured mechanisms for managing data assets effectively. Enterprise Data Management (EDM) has emerged as a crucial discipline that focuses on ensuring data quality, accessibility, security, and compliance across an organization. However, as data governance becomes more critical, organizations face significant challenges in implementing frameworks that align with business objectives while addressing regulatory and technological demands.

Data governance plays a pivotal role in enterprise data management by defining the policies, processes, and standards necessary to ensure data integrity and accountability. A well-structured governance framework helps organizations mitigate risks associated with poor data management, comply with industry regulations, and optimize data-driven decision-making. However, despite its importance, many large organizations struggle with fragmented governance models, data silos, and inconsistent policies, which hinder their ability to extract meaningful insights from their data assets. While existing governance frameworks such as DAMA-DMBOK, COBIT, and CMMI provide structured guidelines, they often lack adaptability to the dynamic needs of large-scale enterprises.

The increasing reliance on emerging technologies such as artificial intelligence (AI), machine learning, cloud computing, and blockchain has further amplified the complexity of data governance. These technologies enable businesses to process and analyze vast datasets in real-time, but they also introduce new challenges related to data security, ethical considerations, and regulatory compliance. Additionally, as global data protection laws become more stringent, organizations must ensure that their governance frameworks align with evolving legal requirements while maintaining operational flexibility.

Despite the availability of established governance models, there remains a gap in practical implementation, particularly in large organizations where multiple departments, stakeholders, and systems operate simultaneously. The lack of a unified, scalable governance approach often results in inefficiencies, compliance risks, and data inconsistencies. As organizations strive to leverage data as a strategic asset, there is an urgent need for a conceptual model that addresses these challenges by offering a structured, adaptable, and business-aligned data governance framework.

This dissertation explores the design of a conceptual model for effective data governance in large enterprises. By examining the key drivers, challenges, and technological advancements shaping data governance, this study aims to bridge the gap between theoretical frameworks and their practical applications. The research will contribute to the development of a governance model that enhances data quality, security, compliance, and overall enterprise data management efficiency.

1.2 Evolution and Importance of Enterprise Data Management

- **The Evolution of Enterprise Data Management and Its Influencing Factors**

Enterprise Data Management (EDM) has undergone significant transformation over the decades, driven by technological advancements, regulatory changes, and the growing importance of data as a strategic asset. Initially, organizations relied on mainframes and relational databases to store structured data with minimal automation. During the 1970s to 1990s, data was managed manually, and governance was largely ignored as organizations focused on storage rather than integration and analytics (Inmon, 1992). The advent of enterprise applications in the early 2000s marked a shift, with the introduction of Enterprise Resource Planning (ERP) and Customer Relationship Management (CRM) systems enabling better data centralization and management. Additionally, the emergence of data warehousing and Business Intelligence (BI) tools allowed organizations to analyze historical data and make informed decisions. The increasing demand for compliance with regulations such as Sarbanes-Oxley Act (SOX, 2002) and Health Insurance Portability and Accountability Act (HIPAA, 1996) further strengthened data governance practices (Kimball & Ross, 2013).

The 2010s witnessed the big data revolution, transforming data management strategies. Technologies like Hadoop, Apache Spark, and NoSQL databases enabled organizations to handle vast volumes of structured and unstructured data efficiently (Jagadish, 2015). Cloud computing platforms, including Amazon Web Services (AWS), Google Cloud, and Microsoft Azure, further revolutionized EDM by offering scalable and cost-effective data storage and processing solutions. Moreover, artificial intelligence (AI) and machine learning began to play a crucial role in predictive analytics and automation of data governance. The introduction of stringent data privacy laws such as the General Data Protection Regulation (GDPR, 2018) and the California Consumer Privacy Act (CCPA, 2020) forced organizations to implement robust data governance frameworks to ensure compliance and protect consumer rights (Zhang et al., 2021).

In the modern EDM landscape (2020s and beyond), organizations are adopting Data Mesh and Data Fabric architectures to ensure seamless integration and decentralized ownership of data. The real-time processing capabilities of technologies like Apache Kafka, Snowflake, and Delta Lake have made it possible for businesses to extract insights in real-time (Dehghani, 2022). AI-driven data management is now a key component of EDM, automating metadata management, data quality control, and governance. Additionally, edge computing and the Internet of Things (IoT) are enabling organizations to process data closer to the source, reducing latency and enhancing efficiency (Gartner, 2023).

Several factors have influenced the evolution of EDM over time. Technology advancements such as AI, cloud computing, and big data analytics have reshaped the way organizations store, access, and analyze data. Regulatory requirements have also played a crucial role, with governments enforcing strict compliance measures to protect data privacy and security. The data explosion—caused by the proliferation of IoT devices, social media, and e-commerce—has necessitated advanced storage and processing capabilities. Moreover, businesses increasingly demand data-driven insights, pushing organizations to prioritize data quality, integration, and governance. Cybersecurity concerns and the rising number of data breaches have further led to the adoption of advanced security measures within data management frameworks. Finally, decentralization and self-service analytics are shifting EDM from an IT-centric model to a business-driven approach, allowing non-technical users to access and analyze data with ease (Seneviratne et al., 2022).

- **Key Principles of Effective Enterprise Data Management and Their Contribution to Organizational Success**

Enterprise Data Management (EDM) is a strategic approach to handling an organization's data assets efficiently. It ensures data accuracy, accessibility, security, and compliance while enabling data-driven decision-making. Effective EDM is built on several key principles that contribute to organizational success by enhancing operational efficiency, regulatory compliance, and business intelligence.

One of the foundational principles of EDM is data governance, which involves defining policies, procedures, and responsibilities for managing data within an organization. A well-structured governance framework ensures data consistency, accountability, and compliance with regulatory requirements such as the General Data Protection Regulation (GDPR) and the California Consumer Privacy Act (CCPA) (Khatri & Brown, 2010). By implementing governance models like DAMA-DMBOK or COBIT, organizations can maintain high data quality, mitigate risks, and align data strategies with business objectives.

Another critical aspect of EDM is data quality management, which ensures that data is accurate, complete, consistent, and timely. Poor data quality can result in incorrect insights, operational inefficiencies, and compliance violations (Redman, 2016). Organizations adopt data cleansing, validation, and enrichment techniques to maintain data integrity. High-quality data improves customer relationship management (CRM), financial reporting, and AI/ML model accuracy, all of which directly impact business performance.

Master Data Management (MDM) plays a vital role in EDM by centralizing and standardizing critical business data such as customer, product, and financial information. MDM eliminates duplicate and inconsistent data, providing a single source of truth across different departments (Loshin, 2018). This helps organizations improve customer experience, streamline supply chain operations, and ensure regulatory compliance.

Ensuring data security and privacy is essential in today's digital landscape. Organizations must protect sensitive information from unauthorized access, cyber threats, and data breaches. EDM incorporates security frameworks such as ISO 27001, NIST, and zero-trust architecture to safeguard data assets (Seneviratne et al., 2022). Implementing encryption, access controls, and multi-factor authentication ensures that only authorized personnel can access critical data.

Strong security practices enhance customer trust, prevent financial losses, and ensure compliance with global regulations.

As businesses utilize multiple data sources, data integration and interoperability become essential for seamless data flow across systems. ETL (Extract, Transform, Load), API-based integrations, and Data Fabrics enable organizations to integrate data from cloud platforms, on-premise databases, and third-party applications (Dreibelbis, 2020). Effective integration supports real-time analytics, automation, and business intelligence (BI), improving decision-making and operational efficiency.

Another key component of EDM is metadata management, which provides essential context for data by describing its source, structure, and usage. Automated metadata management systems improve data discoverability, lineage tracking, and compliance with governance policies (Zeng et al., 2021). Organizations that leverage metadata effectively can streamline data cataloging, improve searchability, and optimize data utilization across teams.

Data lifecycle management is another critical principle, ensuring that data is properly managed from creation to deletion. Organizations implement data retention policies, archiving strategies, and disposal mechanisms to optimize storage and reduce risks (Miloslavskaya & Tolstoy, 2019). Effective lifecycle management helps reduce storage costs, prevent legal risks, and improve data accessibility for business needs.

In today's fast-paced environment, organizations must adopt real-time data processing and analytics to stay competitive. Technologies such as Apache Kafka, Snowflake, and AI-powered analytics platforms enable businesses to derive actionable insights quickly (Gartner, 2023). Real-time data analytics supports applications such as dynamic pricing, fraud detection, and personalized marketing, ultimately increasing revenue and customer satisfaction.

Another emerging trend is data democratization and self-service analytics, where employees across an organization gain access to data without IT dependency. Self-service BI tools like Power BI, Tableau, and Looker empower business users to generate insights independently (Davenport & Bean, 2018). By democratizing data, organizations enhance agility, foster innovation, and improve decision-making at all levels.

Lastly, scalability and cloud adoption are essential for handling the exponential growth of enterprise data. Cloud-based EDM platforms such as AWS, Google Cloud, and Microsoft Azure provide cost-effective, flexible, and resilient data management solutions (Hashem et al., 2015). Cloud adoption enables businesses to handle large datasets, improve disaster recovery, and enhance collaboration across global teams.

By implementing these principles, organizations can achieve multiple benefits. Enhanced decision-making is one of the most significant advantages, as high-quality data leads to accurate business insights and strategic planning. Operational efficiency improves through integrated and standardized data, reducing duplication and streamlining workflows. Regulatory compliance and security frameworks help organizations mitigate risks and avoid legal penalties. Additionally, data democratization and real-time processing allow businesses to adapt quickly to market changes, optimize customer experiences, and drive innovation.

1.3 Key Drivers and Challenges in Data Governance

- **Primary Drivers Influencing the Adoption of Data Governance Frameworks in Large Enterprises**

Data governance frameworks are essential for managing enterprise data effectively, ensuring its quality, security, and compliance. Large enterprises adopt these frameworks in response to multiple drivers, which can be categorized into organizational, technological, and regulatory factors. These forces shape how businesses implement governance models to ensure data integrity and align with strategic goals.

One of the primary organizational drivers for data governance is the need for data-driven decision-making. Modern enterprises generate vast amounts of data from multiple sources, including customer interactions, operations, and supply chains. To maximize the value of this data, organizations implement governance frameworks that enhance business intelligence (BI) and analytics, ensuring that decision-makers rely on high-quality, consistent data (Davenport & Bean, 2018). Without a governance framework, businesses risk making critical decisions based on inaccurate or incomplete data, which can lead to financial and operational inefficiencies.

Another key factor is the pursuit of operational efficiency. Inefficient data management can lead to redundancies, inconsistencies, and poor collaboration across departments. Without standardized governance policies, employees may work with conflicting datasets, leading to errors and inefficiencies. Data governance frameworks help streamline data access, integration, and standardization, reducing operational inefficiencies and ensuring that employees have access to accurate and reliable information (Loshin, 2018). A well-implemented governance model allows organizations to optimize workflows and improve the overall agility of data processes.

Risk management and business continuity also drive the adoption of data governance frameworks. Data-related risks, such as breaches, loss, or mismanagement, can disrupt business operations and result in significant financial and reputational damage. Effective data governance ensures proper access controls, backup strategies, and compliance measures that mitigate these risks and ensure business continuity (Seneviratne et al., 2022). With the increasing frequency of cyberattacks, organizations must have a governance framework in place to minimize the impact of security threats and maintain trust with stakeholders.

Additionally, enterprises recognize that well-governed data can be a monetizable asset. Organizations leverage governance frameworks to improve customer insights, develop personalized services, and create new revenue streams. By ensuring data accuracy and consistency, companies can use analytics and AI more effectively, gaining a competitive edge in the market (Redman, 2016). As a result, businesses that prioritize data governance not only mitigate risks but also unlock new opportunities for innovation and growth.

The rapid growth of big data and artificial intelligence (AI) has made data governance essential. AI-driven data governance automates data cataloging, quality checks, and metadata management, ensuring that data is reliable, accurate, and usable for advanced analytics (Zeng et al., 2021). Without proper governance, AI models risk being trained on biased or inconsistent data, reducing their effectiveness and reliability. Organizations that adopt AI-based governance frameworks can improve automation, reduce human intervention, and enhance data quality.

The widespread adoption of cloud computing and distributed data architectures has also influenced data governance practices. As enterprises shift toward multi-cloud and hybrid-cloud environments, managing data across different platforms has become complex. Governance frameworks help organizations enforce policies, ensure security, and maintain visibility across cloud environments like AWS, Azure, and Google Cloud (Hashem et al., 2015). By implementing cloud governance strategies, businesses can ensure seamless data management across various platforms while complying with industry regulations.

The rise of Data Mesh and Data Fabric architectures has further necessitated robust governance frameworks. Traditional centralized data management models are being replaced by decentralized data ownership approaches, where different teams manage their data domains. Governance frameworks help enforce data access controls, security policies, and data standardization, ensuring consistency across an enterprise-wide data ecosystem (Dehghani, 2022). These modern architectures enable greater flexibility, allowing organizations to scale their data governance strategies more effectively.

Moreover, enterprises increasingly rely on real-time data processing and the Internet of Things (IoT) for critical operations. With billions of connected devices generating data continuously, organizations need governance policies that ensure data integrity, security, and compliance with industry standards (Gartner, 2023). Without governance, real-time analytics platforms could process inaccurate, incomplete, or unauthorized data, leading to flawed business decisions. Businesses that adopt real-time governance frameworks can enhance data reliability and improve response times in decision-making.

One of the strongest drivers of data governance adoption is the increasingly stringent global data protection laws. Governments and regulatory bodies have implemented strict laws to protect consumer data privacy, forcing enterprises to adopt governance frameworks to ensure compliance. Some of the most impactful regulations include:

General Data Protection Regulation (GDPR, 2018) – Enforces strict rules on data privacy and security for EU citizens.

California Consumer Privacy Act (CCPA, 2020) – Provides data privacy rights for California residents.

Health Insurance Portability and Accountability Act (HIPAA, 1996) – Governs the security of healthcare data in the U.S.

Sarbanes-Oxley Act (SOX, 2002) – Ensures financial data integrity for publicly traded companies (Zhang et al., 2021).

Failure to comply with these laws can lead to substantial fines, legal penalties, and reputational damage. Enterprises adopt governance frameworks to maintain audit trails, enforce access controls, and ensure data protection measures.

Beyond government-imposed regulations, many industries have sector-specific compliance requirements. In the financial sector, frameworks such as Basel III, PCI-DSS, and SEC regulations enforce strict data controls. The healthcare sector must comply with HIPAA and the HITECH Act to protect patient data, while e-commerce and retail companies must adhere to GDPR, CCPA, and PCI-DSS to govern customer data security (Dreibelbis, 2020). These sector-specific requirements push organizations to adopt governance models that align with their industry's regulatory landscape.

- **Challenges in Implementing Data Governance and Strategies to Overcome Them**

Data governance is essential for organizations to ensure data quality, security, compliance, and usability. However, implementing an effective data governance framework presents several challenges that organizations must overcome. These challenges fall into organizational, technological, and regulatory categories, each requiring targeted strategies for resolution.

One of the most significant organizational challenges is the lack of executive buy-in and organizational culture. Many organizations view data governance as a technical or compliance issue rather than a strategic business function. Without executive sponsorship, governance initiatives often struggle to gain the necessary funding and commitment from key stakeholders (Davenport & Bean, 2018). To secure executive buy-in, organizations must demonstrate the business value of data governance by linking it to tangible benefits such as risk reduction, regulatory compliance, revenue growth, and operational efficiency. A clear ROI-driven approach and regular communication with leadership can help align governance initiatives with corporate objectives.

Another key organizational challenge is resistance to change among employees. Many employees resist governance policies due to concerns over additional workload, loss of control, or fear of accountability. A lack of awareness about the importance of data governance can lead to poor adherence to governance policies (Redman, 2016). Organizations should invest in employee training programs to build a culture of data accountability. Providing clear role definitions through Data Stewardship programs can help employees understand their responsibilities. Additionally, using change management strategies and demonstrating quick wins can improve acceptance across the organization.

A further organizational challenge is siloed data and lack of collaboration across departments. Data silos occur when different departments maintain separate, inconsistent data sources, leading to poor data integration and inefficiencies. A lack of communication between IT, business, compliance, and analytics teams can further hinder governance efforts (Loshin, 2018). Implementing cross-functional data governance committees can help align goals, standardize policies, and improve communication between teams. Additionally, leveraging centralized data catalogs and metadata management tools ensures that different teams can access and share consistent data.

From a technological standpoint, one of the biggest challenges organizations face is the lack of scalable and flexible data governance tools. Many organizations struggle to implement governance due to outdated legacy systems that lack automation, scalability, and interoperability. Without robust governance tools, data validation, security, and metadata management become inefficient (Hashem et al., 2015). Organizations should invest in modern data governance platforms with capabilities such as automated data lineage tracking, AI-driven data quality management, and real-time compliance monitoring. Cloud-based governance solutions provide scalability, flexibility, and seamless integration with modern data architectures.

Another technological challenge is poor data quality and inconsistent standards. Many governance initiatives fail due to duplicate, outdated, or inaccurate data across different systems. Inconsistent data definitions and quality standards lead to unreliable analytics and reporting (Zeng et al., 2021). Establishing a Master Data Management (MDM) framework helps ensure data consistency, accuracy, and deduplication across multiple systems. Implementing data validation rules, real-time monitoring, and periodic data audits can further improve data quality.

The increasing adoption of multi-cloud, hybrid-cloud, and decentralized data architectures has introduced security and privacy risks. As organizations move towards modern architectures like Data Mesh and Data Fabric, maintaining security and privacy becomes more complex. The risk of unauthorized access, data breaches, and insider threats grows when data is stored across different platforms (Gartner, 2023). To mitigate these risks, organizations should implement Zero-Trust Architecture (ZTA) to enforce strict access controls, encryption, and continuous authentication. Using cloud-native security tools and automated compliance enforcement ensures consistent security policies across environments.

Regulatory and compliance challenges also pose significant obstacles to effective data governance. The increasing complexity of data privacy regulations has made governance more challenging. Enterprises must comply with GDPR, CCPA, HIPAA, PCI-DSS, SOX, and various regional data protection laws. Managing compliance across multiple jurisdictions while ensuring business agility is a major challenge (Zhang et al., 2021). Implementing a Compliance-as-Code approach allows organizations to automate regulatory checks, audit trails, and policy enforcement. Using Data Protection Impact Assessments (DPIAs) and automated consent management ensures continuous compliance with evolving regulations.

Another regulatory challenge is cross-border data transfers and localization requirements. Many countries now mandate data localization laws, requiring businesses to store and process data within national borders. This creates challenges for multinational companies in managing distributed data governance policies (Miloslavskaya & Tolstoy, 2019). Enterprises should adopt geo-specific data governance frameworks with localized cloud storage, region-specific encryption policies, and federated data architectures to comply with cross-border regulations while maintaining operational efficiency.

To successfully implement data governance, organizations must develop a clear data governance strategy that aligns governance initiatives with business goals and regulatory requirements. Defining roles and responsibilities for Data Stewards, Data Owners, and Compliance Officers ensures accountability. Establishing a centralized governance framework while allowing for flexibility in decentralized environments can enhance governance effectiveness.

Organizations should also adopt scalable and AI-driven data governance tools that offer AI-powered metadata management, automated data lineage, and real-time data quality monitoring. Implementing cloud-native governance solutions enables seamless integration across multi-cloud and hybrid environments.

Building a data-centric culture is equally important. Providing employee training and awareness programs improves data accountability, while Data Stewardship programs encourage ownership of data governance policies. Fostering a culture where employees understand the value of data governance leads to better compliance with policies.

Security must also be prioritized by enforcing Privacy-by-Design and Security-by-Design principles. Organizations should implement Zero-Trust security, encryption, and role-based access controls while automating compliance enforcement and regulatory audits to ensure adherence to laws.

Finally, cross-departmental collaboration is crucial. Establishing cross-functional governance committees involving IT, compliance, legal, and business teams promotes unified governance policies. Using centralized data catalogs and data-sharing platforms helps eliminate silos and standardize governance practices across the organization.

1.4 Industry-Specific Considerations and Regulatory Landscape

- **Developing a Data Governance Framework that Balances Industry-Specific Compliance and Business-Driven Data Strategies**

Organizations must implement data governance frameworks that not only ensure regulatory compliance but also support business-driven data strategies to enhance innovation, analytics, and operational efficiency. Achieving this balance requires integrating industry-specific regulations with a flexible governance strategy that aligns with business objectives and evolving data-driven opportunities.

A major challenge in developing a data governance framework is navigating industry-specific compliance mandates. Regulations vary significantly across industries, necessitating tailored governance approaches. In the financial sector, for instance, institutions must comply with GDPR (General Data Protection Regulation), PCI-DSS (Payment Card Industry Data Security Standard), and Basel III, which emphasize data integrity, security, and auditability (Matai, 2022). Meanwhile, in healthcare, HIPAA (Health Insurance Portability and Accountability Act) mandates strict data confidentiality and security measures (Madhavan, 2024). Similarly, logistics and retail enterprises must focus on data quality and ownership to meet compliance requirements while optimizing supply chain operations (Martijn et al., 2015). Therefore, a one-size-fits-all governance approach is ineffective, and organizations must tailor their strategies to meet both regulatory and business needs.

To address this challenge, organizations should adopt a risk-based data governance framework that prioritizes both compliance risks and business opportunities. By integrating compliance requirements into business workflows rather than treating them as standalone constraints, organizations can align governance policies with operational efficiency. One effective approach is leveraging DAMA-DMBoK (Data Management Body of Knowledge) and DCAM (Data Capability Assessment Model) frameworks to embed compliance into business transformation processes while enabling data monetization and AI-driven decision-making (Akokodaripon et al., 2024).

Another critical aspect of balancing compliance and business goals is defining clear data ownership roles. Organizations must assign Data Stewards, Compliance Officers, and Business Data Owners to ensure both regulatory adherence and strategic data utilization. A cross-functional governance committee that includes legal, IT, business leaders, and compliance teams can help establish standardized policies while providing flexibility for business innovation (Dingre, 2023). Implementing role-based access controls (RBAC) ensures that regulated data remains secure while still allowing business teams to leverage insights.

Incorporating automated compliance monitoring is another key strategy. Traditional compliance methods are resource-intensive and often reactive. Organizations should integrate AI-powered data catalogs, metadata management, and real-time audit trails to automate compliance enforcement (Seabolt et al., 2018). Advanced technologies such as blockchain for immutable audit records and machine learning for anomaly detection can further enhance data security and compliance monitoring (Akokodaripon et al., 2024). By automating policy enforcement, businesses can focus more on data-driven decision-making and competitive intelligence.

Organizations also need to ensure that their data governance framework supports innovation. A Data Mesh or Data Fabric approach can be highly effective in modern business environments. Traditional centralized data governance models often restrict agility and real-time decision-making. By contrast, Data Mesh decentralizes data ownership, allowing business teams to manage and access their own datasets while ensuring regulatory controls remain in place (Dehghani, 2022). On the other hand, Data Fabric facilitates real-time integration across multiple environments, ensuring compliance with regulations while supporting AI-driven analytics (Madhavan, 2024).

Ensuring privacy-by-design principles is crucial in data governance. Organizations should implement data anonymization, differential privacy, and synthetic data techniques to allow business-driven insights while minimizing compliance risks (Martijn et al., 2015). Such strategies enable organizations to use customer and financial data for predictive analytics, AI modeling, and business intelligence while remaining fully compliant with GDPR and other privacy regulations (Efunniyi et al., 2024).

Providing self-service analytics with embedded governance controls can further bridge the gap between compliance requirements and business intelligence. Implementing governance-aware BI platforms such as Tableau, Power BI, and cloud-based analytics tools enables users to explore and visualize data securely while ensuring that sensitive information remains protected (Suresh et al., 2024). Features like data lineage tracking, automated redaction of sensitive data, and compliance dashboards ensure that business users have governed access without violating regulatory requirements.

Given that regulatory landscapes and business needs evolve, organizations must adopt a continuous improvement approach to data governance. Regular compliance audits, risk assessments, and governance refinement workshops help organizations stay ahead of emerging regulations and industry trends (Khatri & Brown, 2010). AI-driven compliance monitoring systems can detect unauthorized data access, security breaches, and policy violations in real-time, reducing regulatory risks and maintaining stakeholder trust (Akokodaripon et al., 2024).

1.5 The Role of Technology and Stakeholders in Data Governance

- **The Impact of Emerging Technologies on Data Governance**

Emerging technologies like AI, blockchain, and cloud computing are significantly impacting data governance practices in large enterprises. These technologies offer improved transparency, efficiency, and decision-making processes (Wu, 2024), but also introduce challenges related to data privacy, security, and ethical considerations (Leghemo et al., 2025). AI and machine learning are being used to automate governance tasks, predict compliance risks, and provide real-time auditing, while blockchain ensures data integrity and transparency in distributed environments (Islam, 2024). Cloud computing necessitates adaptive strategies for data governance, including robust classification, access controls, and encryption methods (Achanta, 2023). To address these challenges, organizations are adopting comprehensive frameworks that integrate key governance principles such as transparency, accountability, and regulatory compliance (Leghemo et al., 2025). These frameworks emphasize collaboration between stakeholders, continuous training, and the integration of advanced analytics to enhance governance capabilities and maintain public trust in the face of rapidly evolving technologies (Leghemo et al., 2025).

- **The Role of Stakeholders in Data Governance Implementation**

Successful implementation of data governance frameworks relies on effective stakeholder engagement and clear definition of roles and responsibilities. Key stakeholders include executive sponsors, governance committees, and data stewards (Chukwurah et al., 2024). Their responsibilities encompass establishing policies, ensuring data quality, privacy, and security, and aligning governance efforts with business objectives (Chukwurah et al., 2024). Effective communication channels and tailored engagement strategies are crucial for fostering collaboration among stakeholders (Chukwurah et al., 2024). Stakeholders should participate in developing governance structures, policies, and metrics for success, such as compliance audits and evaluations of fair data practices. Lessons from ERP implementations highlight the importance of managing stakeholder roles and responsibilities to achieve return on investment (Al-Mashari et al., 2016). Challenges in implementation include organizational resistance, technical obstacles, and regulatory compliance, necessitating industry-specific strategies and continuous stakeholder involvement (Chukwurah et al., 2024).

1.6 Ethical, Social, and Security Implications of Data Governance

- **Balancing Security, Compliance, and Ethical Responsibilities**

Organizations can balance data security, regulatory compliance, and ethical responsibilities through several measures. Implementing privacy by design principles is crucial for compliance with regulations like GDPR and HIPAA, reducing risks and costs while improving customer trust (Babu et al., 2020). Robust data governance, proactive security measures, and continuous compliance monitoring are essential for reducing data breaches and maintaining regulatory compliance. In healthcare, encryption, data integrity measures, and secure transfer protocols are key components of data security, particularly for sensitive patient information. The Corporate Digital Responsibility (CDR) framework can help organizations reconcile digital innovation with ethical responsibilities, though it may require significant resource investment (Hartley et al., 2024). Overall, integrating compliance strategies within comprehensive cybersecurity frameworks is necessary to safeguard sensitive information and uphold organizational integrity in the face of evolving regulations and sophisticated cyber threats.

1.7 Need for a Conceptual Model for Effective Data Governance

- **Limitations of Existing Data Governance Frameworks**

Existing data governance frameworks face limitations in addressing the complexities of large organizations, particularly in cloud and inter-organizational contexts. While these frameworks guide Big Data management, they often lack consistency and empirical validation (Al-Badi et al., 2018; Merkus et al., 2023). The rapid growth of data and increasing global distribution of organizations create challenges in managing decentralized structures and diverse data sources. Traditional intra-organizational governance mechanisms struggle to extend across company boundaries, highlighting the need for inter-organizational role models (Jagals, 2021). To address these limitations, researchers propose new conceptual models tailored for large organizations. These include a hub-and-spoke framework for globally distributed entities (Koppichetti, 2023) and empirically validated sets of data governance capabilities (Merkus et al., 2023). Such models aim to balance centralized control with local flexibility, manage distributed data silos, and facilitate effective inter-organizational data exchange.

1.8 Research Problem

In the digital age, large organizations generate and manage vast amounts of data, making Enterprise Data Management (EDM) a critical component of business operations. However, despite recognizing the importance of data governance frameworks, many organizations struggle with their effective implementation. A key challenge is ensuring data quality, security, compliance, and strategic alignment while navigating regulatory complexities, technological advancements, and organizational resistance.

Existing data governance models often fail to address the specific needs of large enterprises, where data is distributed across multiple departments, systems, and geographies. Fragmented governance, lack of standardized processes, and inconsistent data policies lead to poor data quality, inefficiencies, and compliance risks. Additionally, stakeholders—including data managers, IT professionals, and business leaders—frequently disagree on roles, responsibilities, and governance priorities, further complicating implementation efforts.

Moreover, regulatory requirements such as GDPR, HIPAA, and CCPA impose strict data governance mandates, yet organizations often face challenges in achieving full compliance due to legal ambiguities, technological limitations, and high implementation costs. Emerging technologies like AI, machine learning, blockchain, and cloud computing offer potential solutions but require integration into governance frameworks to enhance scalability, automation, and security.

Given these complexities, there is a pressing need for a conceptual model that provides a structured, adaptable, and scalable approach to data governance in large enterprises. This research aims to design and validate such a model, ensuring that it enhances data quality, compliance, operational efficiency, and strategic decision-making while overcoming the barriers that currently hinder successful data governance implementation.

1.9 Purpose of Research

The purpose of this study is to design and evaluate a conceptual model for an effective data governance framework tailored for large organizations. As data continues to grow in volume and complexity, organizations face significant challenges in ensuring data quality, regulatory compliance, security, and strategic alignment. This study aims to bridge the gap between existing governance frameworks and the evolving needs of large enterprises, ensuring that data governance is not only a compliance-driven initiative but also a strategic enabler for decision-making and business growth.

By utilizing a quantitative research approach, this study will employ surveys and statistical analysis to collect and analyze data related to data governance practices, challenges, and outcomes. The research will focus on identifying measurable relationships between data governance frameworks, data quality, compliance, and strategic business performance. The ultimate goal is to provide practical insights and evidence-based recommendations that will help large organizations enhance their data governance strategies, ensuring improved data integrity, security, and overall operational efficiency in an increasingly data-driven world.

1.10 Significance of the Study

In today's data-driven world, effective data governance frameworks are essential for large organizations to manage vast amounts of data efficiently. As businesses increasingly rely on data for decision-making, ensuring data quality, security, compliance, and strategic alignment has become a critical challenge. This study is significant as it addresses these challenges by proposing a conceptual model for data governance that is specifically tailored for large enterprises. By doing so, it contributes both to academic literature and industry best practices, providing a structured approach to enhancing data governance strategies.

A key contribution of this study is its role in improving data quality and regulatory compliance. With the growing pressure from regulations such as GDPR, HIPAA, and CCPA, organizations must establish strong governance policies to protect sensitive data and mitigate risks. This research will provide insights into how a well-structured governance framework can help organizations maintain compliance while ensuring data integrity, accuracy, and security. The proposed model will offer practical solutions to reduce compliance risks and optimize data management practices.

Another important aspect of this study is its quantitative approach, which ensures that findings are backed by empirical data and statistical validation. Unlike many conceptual studies that rely on qualitative insights, this research will collect and analyze real-world data from industry professionals, making the proposed governance framework more practically applicable. The results will offer evidence-based recommendations that organizations can use to enhance their data governance policies and operational efficiency.

Additionally, this study will provide valuable insights for key stakeholders, including Chief Data Officers (CDOs), IT professionals, compliance officers, and business leaders. By understanding stakeholder perceptions of data governance challenges, benefits, and barriers, organizations can foster a culture of accountability and transparency in data management. The findings will help enterprises develop clear roles and responsibilities for governance implementation, ensuring cross-functional collaboration and long-term sustainability.

Furthermore, as organizations adopt emerging technologies such as AI, big data analytics, cloud computing, and blockchain, integrating these advancements into governance frameworks becomes crucial. This study will explore how technology-driven governance models can enhance data security, scalability, and automation while minimizing risks. By addressing these technological challenges, the research aims to bridge the gap between traditional governance approaches and modern digital transformations.

1.11 Research Purpose and Questions

Research Questions:

1. What is the measurable impact of data governance frameworks on data quality in large organizations?
2. What are the critical success factors for implementing data governance frameworks in large organizations?
3. How do stakeholder perceptions influence the adoption and success of data governance frameworks?

CHAPTER II:
REVIEW OF LITERATURE

2.1 Introduction

Enterprise Data Management (EDM) is a crucial component of large organization's operations in today's data-driven world because of the massive volumes of data they generate, process, and store. EDM is the term used to describe the entire collection of rules, practices, and technological tools that guarantee data is securely, reliably, and consistently managed throughout an organization. Effective data governance has emerged as a top priority as companies depend more and more on data for operational effectiveness, compliance, and strategic decision-making.

Data governance is an essential component of enterprise data management, laying the groundwork for data policies, standards, roles, and responsibilities. In addition to allowing organization's to comply with industry-specific standards and regulatory requirements like the CCPA and GDPR, a well-structured data governance framework guarantees data quality, security, compliance, and accountability. However, there are obstacles to implementing data governance in large organizations, such as stakeholder alignment, scalability problems, integration difficulties, and data divisions.

Organization's still have difficulty creating a conceptual model that combines enterprise-wide data management strategies with governance best practices, even with the existence of numerous data governance frameworks like DAMAD, COBIT, and ISO 38500. There has never been a more pressing need for a strong, flexible, and scalable data governance model, particularly as emerging technologies like artificial intelligence (AI), cloud computing, and real-time analytics transform data management procedures.

The purpose of this review of the literature is to examine the body of knowledge regarding enterprise data management, data governance frameworks, and conceptual models. It also aims to identify any gaps in the literature and suggest a new conceptual model for efficient data governance in big businesses. In order to give organisations a thorough grasp of how to create and maintain an efficient data governance framework, it will look at important issues, industry best practices, and new developments.

2.2 EDM Impact on BI & Decision-Making and Challenges in EDM Implementation

- **EDM Impact on BI & Decision-Making**

Business intelligence (BI) and decision-making are greatly impacted by enterprise data management methods, which use big data analytics. Businesses utilise business intelligence (BI) to improve decision-making by extracting insights from both structured and unstructured data (Herschel, 2021). Nonetheless, obstacles like inadequate data quality and privacy issues call for efficient data management techniques like Master Data Management (Herschel, 2021). By tackling problems like plan failure and risk-taking capabilities, the Optimised Data Management using Big Data Analytics (ODM-BDA) framework improves organisational performance and decision-making (Niu et al., 2021). Context-specific data transformation procedures that include static and dynamic assessments for holistic intelligence are essential components of critical business intelligence (BI) operations (Mathrani, 2021). These procedures differ from company to company, reflecting obstacles and areas for development (Mathrani, 2021). In the end, BI is crucial for gathering, analysing, and verifying both internal and external data in order to produce specialised knowledge that affects choices (Negro & Mesia, 2020).

2.3 Challenges in EDM Implementation

Organizations encounter several significant obstacles when it comes to implementing Enterprise Data Management. Among these, policy-related challenges are particularly pronounced, especially in the healthcare sector (Shinta Oktaviana R. et al., 2024). Issues related to data management, such as quality, ownership, and accessibility, are also prevalent (Shinta Oktaviana R. et al., 2024; Athira M. Nambiar & Divyansh Mundra, 2022). Crucial barriers include engagement from leadership, clearly defined roles and responsibilities, and the allocation of suitable budgets (R. Chakravorty, 2020). Companies face difficulties in fostering a data-centric culture and developing effective communication strategies (R. Chakravorty, 2020). The vast volume and diversity of big data create complications in both management and analysis (Athira M. Nambiar & Divyansh Mundra, 2022). Moreover, the challenges encountered may differ depending on the market segment and the country in which an organization operates (C. Bassi & S. Alves-Souza, 2023). Addressing these challenges is vital for the effective implementation of data governance initiatives and for leveraging organizational data to enhance decision-making and secure a competitive edge.

2.4 Data Architecture & EDM Relationship and Critical Success Factors

- **Data Architecture & EDM Relationship**

Data architecture and Enterprise Data Management (EDM) are fundamentally linked in large enterprises. The architecture of EDM is essential for linking distributed campuses and coordinating actions across organizations (Fajar Mahardika & R. Sumantri, 2020). The dynamic between Chief Data Officers (CDOs) and Enterprise Architects (EAs) is crucial for achieving agility in enterprise data, with a suggested model spanning from isolated functions to a comprehensive enterprise strategy (Kaddoumi & Tambo, 2023). Scalable data architectures, such as data lakes and warehouses, are critical for managing a variety of data sources and workloads within enterprise data platforms (Ashraf, 2023). These data management systems are vital for contemporary enterprise data management, differing in their characteristics and uses while supporting effective big data analytics (Nambiar & Mundra, 2022). The combination of data architecture and EDM enhances decision-making, provides a competitive edge, and promotes the optimal use of organizational information in large enterprises.

- **Critical Success Factors in Data Governance**

Data governance frameworks are crucial for effectively executing data-driven decision-making in organizations. Essential factors for successful data governance include ensuring data integrity, creating control mechanisms, and considering legal aspects (Chandra et al., 2023; Bhatia & Kumar, 2020). Properly implemented data governance allows for the standardization, accessibility, and analysis of data to produce actionable insights (Bento et al., 2022). Key technological components encompass data storage, sharing, archiving, and preservation (Chandra et al., 2023). Organizations must ensure their data governance is in harmony with organizational, technological, and analytical aspects (Al-Sai et al., 2020). A comprehensive data governance framework should address five main domains: organization, technology, personnel, data management, and governance (Al-Sai et al., 2020). Sustainability plays a crucial role in the long-term success of data governance efforts, requiring an all-encompassing approach (Bento et al., 2022). By embracing these key success factors, organizations can overcome challenges in big data analytics and implementation, leading to enhanced data-driven decision-making (Al-Sai et al., 2020; Bhatia & Kumar, 2020).

2.5 Barriers to Effective Data Governance and Implications of Poor Data Governance

- **Barriers to Effective Data Governance**

Implementing effective data governance in large enterprises faces many obstacles. According to Madhavan (2024) and Chukwurah et al. (2024), these include organisational issues such ambiguous roles and duties, low stakeholder participation, and the requirement for a data-driven culture. Problems with data quality, security, and integrating new technologies like blockchain and artificial intelligence are examples of technical challenges (Madhavan, 2024; Styrin, 2023). Other challenges include changing privacy regulations and regulatory compliance (Chukwurah et al., 2024). Progress is also hampered by cultural constraints like low digital trust among citizens and inadequate data literacy among staff and the general public (Styrin, 2023). There are issues unique to certain industries, such as manufacturing, healthcare, and finance (Chukwurah et al., 2024). It will take a comprehensive framework that tackles risk management, standardisation, and policy development to overcome these obstacles (Madhavan, 2024; Bassi & Alves-Souza, 2023). For data governance to be implemented successfully, certain issues must be prioritised (Bassi & Alves-Souza, 2023).

- **Implications of Poor Data Governance**

Business operations and regulatory compliance can be greatly impacted by inadequate data governance. When it comes to the gathering, storing, and sharing of data, inadequate governance systems may have ethical and legal repercussions (Sharma et al., 2022). Complex regulatory environments are difficult for organisations to navigate, especially when dealing with cross-border situations where data security and privacy laws differ (Coche et al., 2023). To reduce risks, preserve data integrity, and guarantee regulatory compliance, strong data governance systems are essential (Adebayo et al., 2024). Effective data governance is crucial for disaster recovery and business continuity in cloud-based systems, necessitating that organisations manage vendor relationships, put robust security measures in place, and comply with industry-specific laws like PCI-DSS and HIPAA (Rakshith & Pawar, 2024). An organization's capacity to function effectively and uphold compliance may be impacted by regulatory loopholes, unclear benchmarking procedures, and heightened susceptibility to data breaches resulting from improper data governance (Sharma et al., 2022; Coche et al., 2023).

2.6 Cloud Computing & Data Governance in EDM and Role of Automation in Compliance & Data Integrity

- **Cloud Computing & Data Governance in EDM**

Enterprise data management and governance have been profoundly impacted by cloud computing, requiring organisations to adopt flexible ways (Achanta, 2023). Data classification, encryption, access restrictions, and lifecycle management are important factors to take into account in order to address compliance and data residency issues (Achanta, 2023). A comprehensive strategy that integrates management and technical viewpoints is necessary for data security in cloud-based governance (Liu, 2022). The establishment, upkeep, and sustainability of enterprise data warehouses for research (EDW4R) in clinical and translational contexts are difficult, and cloud migration offers both advantages and disadvantages (Knosp et al., 2022). The integration of big data with cloud computing offers scalability, flexibility, and cost-effectiveness for data processing and analysis. But it also brings with it issues with data migration, privacy, security, governance, skill requirements, vendor lock-in, and compliance (Sandhu, 2021). To optimise the potential of big data in cloud environments, future research themes include privacy-preserving analysis, edge computing integration, better analytics, and industry-specific applications (Sandhu, 2021).

- **Role of Automation in Compliance & Data Integrity**

In governance frameworks, automation is essential for maintaining data integrity and compliance. Data accuracy, consistency, and security can be greatly enhanced by AI-driven data quality management and automated procedures (Desani, 2023; Manigonda, 2023). Predictive compliance risk assessment, automated auditing, and real-time monitoring are made possible by these technologies (Islam, 2024). Without requiring human involvement, automated data contracts and smart contract technology enforce data usage guidelines and regulatory compliance (Desani, 2023). Centralised dashboard implementation improves data governance decision-making and transparency (Manigonda, 2023). Data integrity and transparency are further strengthened when blockchain, AI, and machine learning are integrated into cloud-based systems (Islam, 2024). Strong data governance frameworks are necessary to reduce risks, preserve data integrity, and make regulatory compliance easier (Adebayo et al., 2024). Organisations can overcome the difficulties of managing massive datasets in a regulatory environment that is becoming more complex by utilising automation to create data governance frameworks that are more effective, scalable, and sustainable (Manigonda, 2023; Islam, 2024).

- **Technology & Automation in Governance Efficiency**

Technology and automation are revolutionizing corporate governance and public service delivery, enhancing efficiency, transparency, and effectiveness. Board management, risk assessment, and legal compliance are just a few of the governance procedures that are using AI and automation (Locke & Bird, 2020). Performance metrics and managerial efficacy can be enhanced by automating corporate governance operations as business processes (Endutkin, 2020). With many nations implementing digital governance frameworks, AI and automation in public services are meeting the growing demands and expectations of citizens (Neupane, 2023). Technological developments are enabling decentralised governance through smart contracts and DAOs, revolutionising shareholder voting through blockchain, and rethinking information asymmetry (Jiang & Li,

2024). The adoption of ethical AI, the digital gap, and possible new inequities are still obstacles, nevertheless (Neupane, 2023; Jiang & Li, 2024). In addition to investments in digital infrastructure and capacity building, cooperation between scholars, policymakers, and practitioners is essential to maximising the benefits of technology in governance (Neupane, 2023; Jiang & Li, 2024).

2.7 Data Governance Models and Emerging Trends & Best Practices

Several methodologies can be used to evaluate and measure the success of conceptual models for data governance. Schmuck and Georgescu (2024) suggest modifying the Information Systems Success Measurement Model by DeLone and McLean in order to evaluate the efficacy of data governance. In order to improve data quality, Karkosková (2022) offers a Data Governance Model designed specifically for financial organisations and based on BCBS 239 and DAMA methodology. In order to assess the effectiveness of e-learning systems, Riandi et al. (2021) propose a conceptual model that uses user satisfaction as a mediator between the quality of the system and e-learning services and the performance of individual students. In their discussion of blockchain technology and artificial intelligence's potential to increase governance transparency, Alshamsi et al. (2020) highlight conceptual modelling as the best strategy. These studies emphasise how crucial it is to modify current frameworks, add industry-specific specifications, take user satisfaction into account, and make use of cutting-edge technology in order to create useful conceptual models for assessing the performance of data governance.

Recent research highlights emerging trends and best practices in data governance. The role of public authorities and civic society in democratising data governance is highlighted by the identification of four types of data governance: data sharing pools, data cooperatives, public data trusts, and personal data sovereignty (Micheli et al., 2020). While addressing issues in a variety of businesses, effective frameworks for data governance emphasise the significance of strong policies, procedures, and measurements (Chukwurah et al., 2024). Blockchain, AI, and machine learning are being utilised more and more in cloud-based big data analytics to automate governance duties, anticipate compliance risks, and guarantee data integrity (Islam, 2024). Maintaining constant data quality, putting multi-layered security measures in place, and cultivating close cooperation with cloud service providers are examples of best practices (Islam,

2024; Pansara, 2021). These tactics seek to improve decision-making, guarantee adherence to regulations, and unleash the complete potential of data assets throughout enterprises (Chukwurah et al., 2024; Pansara, 2021).

2.8 Future Regulatory Impact on EDM & Data Governance and Business Value & Competitive Advantage of Data Governance

- **Future Regulatory Impact**

Enterprise data governance is critical for organisations seeking to maximise data value while minimising risks and ensuring compliance (Madhavan, 2024). Clear policies, roles, and quality standards are also components of effective frameworks (Chukwurah et al., 2024). Maintaining data integrity, reducing risk, and complying with regulations all depend on strong data governance frameworks (Adebayo et al., 2024). Stakeholder involvement, technological integration, and industry-specific tactics are important elements (Chukwurah et al., 2024). Big data and analytics present ethical, privacy, and security issues in addition to prospects for corporate advantage (Yallop & Séraphin, 2020). Future difficulties include adjusting to changing laws, incorporating AI and machine learning, and dealing with large data and Internet of Things-related concerns (Chukwurah et al., 2024). To incorporate more efficient privacy and ethics solutions, organisations need to go beyond compliance-based frameworks (Yallop & Séraphin, 2020). Successful implementation requires a comprehensive strategy that supports a data-driven culture and is in line with organisational goals (Madhavan, 2024).

- **Business Value & Competitive Advantage of Data Governance**

Effective data governance enhances company value and competitive advantage by guaranteeing data correctness, security, and integrity (Koilakonda, 2024). It improves overall competitiveness, decision-making skills, and organisational agility (Koilakonda, 2024; Black et al., 2023). However, there are obstacles to putting data governance into practice, including cultural considerations, strategy creation, and leadership involvement (Chakravorty, 2020). By recognising data as a strategic asset, facilitating better-informed decision-making, and preventing potential litigation, a methodical data governance framework can enhance outcomes (Huff & Lee, 2020). Boards are essential in determining risk tolerance and managing the data assets' risk/reward trade-off (Black et al., 2023). Better information quality, lower expenses, more output, and higher performance across a range of corporate operations can all result from effective data governance (Huff & Lee, 2020). In an increasingly data-driven environment, data governance is crucial for organisations to leverage data as a critical mechanism for competitive advantage (Black et al., 2023; Huff & Lee, 2020).

- **Data-Driven Culture & Governance Policies**

Organization's must overcome a number of obstacles in order to establish a data-driven culture with robust governance practices. In order to improve organizational performance and create a data-driven culture (DDC), data governance (DG) is essential (Fattah, 2024; Burton, 2021). Establishing successful DG programs, improving data literacy proficiency, and putting in place trustworthy decision-making mechanisms are crucial components (Bassi et al., 2024; Fattah, 2024; Biagi & Russo, 2022). To close the gap between data availability and utilization, organizations should concentrate on the four pillars of data governance, each of which has six essential aspects (Burton, 2021). Rapid data collection and transformation from many sources can be facilitated by a data model architecture that supports the deployment of data-driven IT governance (Biagi & Russo, 2022). Raising DG maturity and becoming truly data-driven need addressing issues with organizational culture and data governance (Bassi et al., 2024). Organizations can develop a data-driven culture that improves customer acquisition, retention, and profitability by giving priority to certain factors (Burton, 2021).

2.9 Data Governance Models & Cyber-security

Data governance frameworks are critical in preventing data breaches and reducing cyber-security risks for organization's. Policies, processes, and technology that complement overarching cyber-security goals are all part of effective data governance frameworks (Kumar et al., 2024). By addressing important components including data classification, access management, and real-time monitoring, these frameworks improve resilience (Kumar et al., 2024). Cyber hazards can be managed without the need for onerous regulatory requirements by putting strong data governance processes into place (Rajaretnam, 2020). Organization's can create effective cyber-security solutions by using quantitative assessment models to evaluate breach costs and likelihood (Algarni et al., 2021). The Data Management Association (DAMA) International Guide establishes a conceptual framework for long-term data governance, emphasizing the importance of information security in maintaining data confidentiality, integrity, and availability (Aguboshim et al., 2023). Organization's can improve their overall cyber-security posture by utilizing data governance programs to guarantee regulated access to secure data across all of their systems (Aguboshim et al., 2023).

2.10 Literature Gaps

Despite extensive research on Enterprise Data Management (EDM) and Data Governance Frameworks, several critical gaps remain that hinder the development of a comprehensive, scalable, and adaptable governance model for large organizations. The literature review highlights various frameworks, challenges, and best practices, but the following gaps persist:

1. Lack of a Unified Conceptual Model for Large Organizations

While multiple data governance frameworks exist (e.g., DAMA, COBIT, ISO 38500), there is no **comprehensive and adaptable conceptual model** tailored for large organizations. Existing models often focus on **specific industries or regulatory compliance** but fail to provide a **holistic approach** that integrates governance best practices with enterprise-wide data management strategies.

2. Limited Empirical Validation of Data Governance Impact

Many studies discuss the importance of data governance in ensuring **data quality, compliance, and security**, but **few offer quantitative validation** of its direct impact on **business intelligence, decision-making, and operational efficiency**. Most research relies on **theoretical discussions or case studies**, lacking **data-driven insights** to assess governance effectiveness.

3. Challenges in Implementing Data Governance in Large, Complex Organizations

Existing literature highlights common challenges in data governance, such as **stakeholder alignment, data silos, and technological integration**, yet there is **limited research on overcoming these barriers** in large enterprises. The absence of a **practical, step-by-step implementation framework** makes it difficult for organizations to establish **scalable and sustainable governance structures**.

4. Insufficient Focus on Emerging Technologies in Data Governance

While research acknowledges the growing role of **AI, big data analytics, block-chain, and cloud computing** in data governance, **there is a lack of studies exploring how these technologies can be systematically integrated** into governance models. The literature does not fully address **how automation, predictive analytics, and AI-driven compliance tools** can enhance governance efficiency and adaptability.

2.11 Summary

The literature review explores the critical role of Enterprise Data Management (EDM) and Data Governance Frameworks in large organizations, emphasizing their significance in ensuring data quality, security, compliance, and strategic decision-making. It highlights the increasing reliance on data-driven insights and the need for a structured governance framework to manage the complexity and volume of enterprise data effectively.

The review examines how EDM influences Business Intelligence (BI) and decision-making, demonstrating that organizations leveraging big data analytics and optimized data management frameworks experience enhanced decision-making capabilities. However, challenges such as poor data quality, lack of standardization, and fragmented governance structures hinder the full potential of data-driven strategies.

Additionally, the relationship between data architecture and EDM is discussed, emphasizing the need for scalable data infrastructures such as data lakes and warehouses to support governance initiatives. The review also identifies critical success factors in data governance, such as data integrity, standardization, compliance mechanisms, and stakeholder engagement, which are essential for ensuring effective governance implementation.

Despite the availability of existing data governance models like DAMA, COBIT, and ISO 38500, organizations continue to face barriers in implementation, including stakeholder resistance, lack of technological integration, and evolving regulatory requirements. The review also underscores the implications of poor data governance, which can lead to data breaches, regulatory non-compliance, and operational inefficiencies.

Emerging technologies such as AI, blockchain, automation, and cloud computing present new opportunities for strengthening data governance. However, the review finds limited research on how to systematically integrate these technologies into governance models. Additionally, challenges related to regulatory adaptation, industry-specific governance needs, and quantifiable measurement of governance effectiveness remain unresolved.

CHAPTER III:
METHODOLOGY

3.1 Overview of the Research Problem

Large organizations face significant challenges in managing vast data efficiently while ensuring data quality, security, and regulatory compliance. As data-driven decision-making becomes increasingly crucial, organizations must establish robust data governance frameworks to maintain consistency, accuracy, and compliance with regulations such as GDPR and HIPAA. However, implementing these frameworks is often resisted due to organizational culture, lack of expertise, and resource constraints. Many enterprises struggle with legacy systems that hinder seamless data integration, leading to inefficiencies and increased risks of data breaches. Additionally, aligning data governance strategies with business objectives remains complex, requiring structured methodologies to measure their impact on data quality and business outcomes. The growing adoption of emerging technologies, such as artificial intelligence, machine learning, and blockchain, offers potential solutions and introduces new complexities. This research aims to address these challenges by developing a conceptual model tailored for large organizations, focusing on the measurable impact of data governance frameworks on data quality and strategic business performance. Using a quantitative approach, the study seeks to identify critical success factors, analyze stakeholder perceptions, and provide data-driven insights to improve governance practices. The findings will help organizations enhance their data management strategies, streamline operations, and leverage data governance for better decision-making and long-term growth.

3.2 Operationalization of Theoretical Constructs

Operationalizing theoretical constructs in this research involves defining key variables related to data governance frameworks and their measurable impact on data quality and strategic business outcomes in large organizations. The study focuses on data quality improvement, business outcomes enhancement, decision-making effectiveness, strategic alignment, and process optimization. These constructs are quantified through survey responses from key stakeholders, including data managers, IT professionals, and business analysts, ensuring a structured approach to data measurement. Statistical methods, including regression analysis and correlation tests, assess relationships between these variables and identify significant predictors of effective data governance. For instance, data quality improvement is operationalized by evaluating accuracy, consistency, and reliability metrics reported by respondents. Business outcomes enhancement is measured through factors like operational efficiency and financial performance, while decision-making effectiveness is assessed based on access to accurate and timely data. The study also considers strategic alignment by examining how well data governance practices integrate with organizational goals. By applying a quantitative approach, this research ensures that theoretical constructs are translated into measurable indicators, allowing for objective analysis and actionable insights that can support organizations in optimizing their data governance frameworks.

3.3 Research Purpose and Questions

Purpose

This research aims to evaluate the impact of data governance frameworks on data quality and strategic business outcomes in large organizations. As organizations generate vast amounts of data, ensuring its accuracy, security, and compliance with regulatory standards has become a critical challenge. This study aims to identify the key factors contributing to the successful implementation of data governance frameworks and assess stakeholder perceptions regarding their benefits, challenges, and barriers. By employing a quantitative approach, the research seeks to provide empirical evidence on how governance practices influence data management efficiency and business decision-making.

Research Questions:

The study is guided by three primary research questions:

- What is the measurable impact of data governance frameworks on data quality in large organizations?

- What are the critical success factors for implementing data governance frameworks?
- How do stakeholder perceptions influence the adoption and success of data governance frameworks?

Addressing these questions will provide valuable insights into best practices for organizations seeking to enhance their data governance strategies, optimize decision-making processes, and ensure long-term compliance and efficiency.

3.4 Research Design

This research adopts a **quantitative** design to systematically analyze the impact of data governance frameworks on data quality and strategic business outcomes in large organizations. The study employs a structured survey method to collect primary data from key stakeholders, including data managers, IT professionals, and business analysts. These surveys consist of closed-ended questions to measure data quality improvement, business process efficiency, decision-making effectiveness, and regulatory compliance. The collected data is analyzed using statistical techniques, including **regression analysis and correlation tests**, to identify relationships between governance practices and organizational performance. By focusing solely on numerical data, this research ensures objectivity and replicability in assessing governance frameworks.

Additionally, factor analysis is applied to determine the most influential success factors in implementing effective governance strategies. The research design ensures that findings are based on empirical evidence, providing actionable insights organizations can use to enhance their data governance models. This structured approach allows for a rigorous evaluation of governance effectiveness, supporting data-driven decision-making in large enterprises.

3.5 Impact of Data Governance on Data Quality & Business Outcomes

Objective

• To statistically evaluate the relationship between the implementation of data governance frameworks and the improvement in data quality and strategic business outcomes within large organizations.

Methodology

The methodology for objective one involves a quantitative approach to statistically evaluate the relationship between the implementation of data governance frameworks and improvements in data quality and strategic business outcomes within large organizations. Data was collected through a structured online survey targeting key stakeholders, including data managers, IT professionals, business analysts, and executives. The survey consisted of closed-ended questions using a Likert scale to measure perceptions of governance effectiveness, data quality, and business performance. The responses were analyzed using statistical methods, including regression analysis and correlation tests, to identify the strength and significance of relationships between governance practices and organizational outcomes. Descriptive statistics were used to summarize the demographic characteristics of the participants, ensuring a diverse and representative sample. Factor analysis was applied to group governance elements and determine their relative impact on data quality and business efficiency. By employing a structured and objective data analysis process, this methodology ensures that findings are based on empirical evidence, providing actionable insights for organizations seeking to optimize their data governance strategies.

3.6 Key Success Factors for Data Governance Implementation

Objective

• To identify and prioritize the critical factors that contribute to the successful implementation of data governance frameworks in large organizations.

Methodology

The methodology for objective two follows a quantitative approach to identify and prioritize the critical factors contributing to the successful implementation of data governance frameworks in large organizations. Data was collected through a structured online survey distributed to key stakeholders, including data managers, IT professionals, business analysts, and executives, ensuring diverse industry representation. The survey included closed-ended questions using a Likert scale to measure the perceived importance and impact of various governance factors. Statistical techniques such as factor analysis and regression analysis were employed to determine which factors had the most significant influence on governance success. Factor analysis helped categorize governance elements into meaningful dimensions, while regression analysis identified the extent to which these factors contributed to overall governance effectiveness. Additionally, correlation analysis was conducted to assess the relationships between governance success factors and organizational performance metrics. This structured methodology ensures that findings are data-driven, allowing organizations to focus on the most impactful governance components to enhance data management and business outcomes.

3.7 Stakeholder Perceptions on Data Governance

Objective

- To evaluate the perceptions of stakeholders regarding the benefits, challenges, and barriers to adopting data governance frameworks in large organizations.

Methodology

The methodology for objective three employs a quantitative approach to evaluate stakeholder perceptions regarding the benefits, challenges, and barriers to adopting data governance frameworks in large organizations. Data was collected using a structured online survey distributed to key stakeholders, including data managers, IT professionals, business analysts, and executives, ensuring a representative sample across different industries. The survey contained closed-ended questions based on a Likert scale, allowing participants to express their level of agreement with statements related to data governance's effectiveness, challenges, and barriers. Descriptive statistics analyzed stakeholder responses and identified perception trends across different organizational roles and industries. Correlation analysis was applied to explore the relationships between stakeholder perceptions and governance outcomes, providing insights into how different groups view the adoption and impact of governance practices. Additionally, factor analysis was conducted to classify common themes in governance perceptions, helping to identify key areas of concern and opportunities for improvement. This structured approach ensures that findings are based on empirical data, allowing organizations to address challenges and refine governance strategies for improved adoption and effectiveness.

3.8 Population and Sample

The population for this research consists of professionals involved in data management, governance, and decision-making within large organizations. This includes data managers, IT professionals, business analysts, compliance officers, and executives crucial in implementing and overseeing data governance frameworks. The study focuses on large organizations across multiple industries, including finance, healthcare, technology, and manufacturing, where data governance is critical to operational success.

A sample of 255 participants was selected using a structured survey approach to ensure diverse representation across different organizational levels and industries. The sample includes professionals from senior management, representing 33.7 per cent; executive roles at 33.3 per cent; mid-level management at 26.7 per cent; and entry-level positions at 6.3 per cent, providing a broad perspective on governance practices. The industry distribution indicates that 39.2 per cent of respondents are from the finance sector, 20.4 per cent from healthcare, 16.9 per cent from technology, and smaller proportions from the manufacturing and retail sectors.

The study ensures that the sample is representative of large organizations where data governance is actively implemented, allowing for robust statistical analysis. Including professionals with varying levels of experience and responsibility provides a well-rounded understanding of how governance frameworks influence data quality, business outcomes, and decision-making processes. The sample size and diversity enable the research to generate generalizable insights that can be applied to organizations seeking to enhance their data governance strategies.

3.9 Participant Selection

The participants for this research were selected based on their roles and involvement in data management and governance activities within large organizations. The study targeted key stakeholders, including data managers, IT professionals, business analysts, compliance officers, and executives, with direct experience and knowledge of implementing and maintaining data governance frameworks. These participants were chosen to ensure a comprehensive understanding of how governance practices impact data quality, business outcomes, and decision-making processes across different organizational levels. The selection process focused on professionals from diverse industries, including finance, healthcare, technology, and manufacturing, where data governance plays a critical role in operational success.

Participants were invited to participate in a structured online survey to capture quantitative data and stakeholder insights. The survey included a mix of closed-ended questions to ensure standardized responses, which would facilitate statistical analysis. To achieve broad representation, outreach was made to professionals across various levels of seniority, including senior management, mid-level management, and entry-level roles. This approach ensured that the data reflects diverse perspectives and experiences with governance implementation. By targeting participants who are directly engaged with data governance practices, the research aims to generate reliable and actionable insights that can be applied to strengthen governance strategies in large organizations.

3.10 Instrumentation

The research utilizes a structured survey as the primary instrument for data collection, designed to measure the impact of data governance frameworks on data quality and strategic business outcomes in large organizations. The survey comprises closed-ended questions to ensure standardized responses, facilitating quantitative analysis. It captures key variables such as data quality improvement, enhancement of business outcomes, decision-making effectiveness, strategic alignment, and optimization of business processes. The instrument was developed based on established data governance frameworks and prior research in enterprise data management to ensure validity and reliability.

To assess the relationships between governance practices and organizational performance, the survey includes Likert-scale questions that allow participants to express their level of agreement with various statements related to governance effectiveness. Additionally, demographic questions were included to capture participant characteristics such as industry, organizational role, years of experience, and company size. Statistical techniques, including regression analysis and correlation tests, were applied to analyze the collected responses, identifying key success factors in governance implementation. The structured nature of the survey ensures that the data remains objective, replicable, and suitable for empirical evaluation. By employing a rigorous survey-based approach, the study aims to provide actionable insights into optimizing data governance strategies within large organizations.

3.11 Data Collection Procedures

The data collection procedure for this research followed a structured and systematic approach to ensure the accuracy and reliability of findings. The study utilized an online survey method to gather quantitative data from key stakeholders, including data managers, IT professionals, business analysts, compliance officers, and executives within large organizations. The survey was designed to assess the impact of data governance frameworks on data quality, business outcomes, decision-making effectiveness, and strategic alignment. It consisted of closed-ended questions with a Likert-scale format, allowing respondents to indicate their level of agreement with statements related to governance effectiveness, business performance, and regulatory compliance.

Participants were selected using a targeted outreach approach, ensuring representation from diverse industries, including finance, healthcare, technology, and manufacturing. The survey was distributed via email invitations and professional networks, maximizing participation from professionals with direct experience in data governance implementation. To enhance response rates, reminders were sent periodically, and participants were assured of confidentiality to encourage honest and unbiased responses.

Once responses were collected, the data underwent cleaning and validation to remove incomplete or inconsistent entries, ensuring the dataset was suitable for analysis. The cleaned data was then analyzed using statistical methods such as regression analysis and correlation tests to identify key success factors and measure the relationships between governance practices and organizational performance. This structured data collection process ensured the research remained quantitative, objective, and replicable, providing valuable insights for improving data governance frameworks in large organizations.

3.12 Data Analysis

The data analysis for this research was conducted using statistical methods to evaluate the impact of data governance frameworks on data quality and strategic business outcomes in large organizations. Once the survey data was collected, thorough data cleaning and validation were performed to remove incomplete or inconsistent responses, ensuring accuracy and reliability. The cleaned dataset was then analyzed using descriptive statistics to summarize the demographic distribution of participants, including age, gender, industry, job role, and organizational size. These statistics provided an overview of the respondent characteristics, ensuring that the sample was representative of large organizations implementing data governance frameworks.

Regression analysis and correlation tests were applied to examine the relationships between key governance variables. Regression analysis determined how independent variables, such as data quality improvement, business outcomes enhancement, decision-making effectiveness, and business process optimization, influenced dependent variables like governance success and strategic alignment. The results provided statistical evidence on which factors strongly impacted governance effectiveness. Correlation analysis was conducted to measure the strength and direction of relationships between different governance components, helping to identify key success factors.

The findings showed a significant positive relationship between governance frameworks and improvements in data quality, business outcomes, and decision-making processes. Statistical tests indicated that improvement in business outcomes had the most decisive influence on data quality, highlighting the importance of aligning governance strategies with organizational goals. Other factors contributed significantly, such as enhancement of decision-making and improvements in post-governance quality. The analysis further revealed that governance effectiveness varied by industry, with finance and healthcare sectors showing the highest levels of governance implementation.

Additionally, factor analysis was conducted to identify underlying dimensions within the dataset, helping to group governance-related components into meaningful categories. This technique gave a more precise evaluation of which governance elements contributed most to organizational success. The results provided empirical support for the effectiveness of data governance frameworks, offering actionable insights that organizations can use to strengthen governance strategies. By employing a structured, quantitative approach, the data analysis ensured objective, data-driven conclusions that contribute to advancing best practices in enterprise data management.

3.13 Research Design Limitations

While structured to provide a quantitative and objective analysis of data governance frameworks, the research design has certain limitations that must be acknowledged. One key limitation is the reliance on self-reported survey data, which may introduce response bias. Participants' perceptions and interpretations of data governance effectiveness could be influenced by their individual experiences, leading to potential subjectivity despite the structured nature of the survey. Additionally, the study focuses on large organizations, limiting the generalizability of findings to small and medium-sized enterprises, which may have different governance challenges and resource constraints.

Another limitation is the cross-sectional nature of the data collection, which captures responses at a single point in time. This approach does not allow for tracking long-term changes in governance effectiveness or identifying causal relationships between governance frameworks and business outcomes. While regression analysis helps establish correlations, it cannot definitively prove causation. Furthermore, the study primarily uses survey-based metrics, which, although statistically analyzed, may not capture all the complexities of governance implementation, such as cultural resistance, evolving regulatory requirements, and technological advancements.

Additionally, while diverse across industries, the study sample may have uneven representation from different sectors, as finance and healthcare organizations had a higher proportion of responses. This could lead to an overemphasis on governance practices that are more prevalent in these industries, potentially overlooking sector-specific challenges in fields like manufacturing or retail. Lastly, while the research employs robust statistical techniques, the findings are limited to the variables included in the survey, meaning other external factors influencing governance success may not be accounted for.

Despite these limitations, the study provides valuable empirical insights into the effectiveness of data governance frameworks in large organizations. Future research could address these constraints by incorporating longitudinal studies, industry-specific analyses, or complementary qualitative methods to deepen understanding of governance impacts across various business environments.

3.14 Conclusion

The findings of this research highlight the significant role of data governance frameworks in improving data quality, business outcomes, and decision-making processes in large organizations. The quantitative analysis confirms that well-implemented governance strategies lead to measurable improvements in data accuracy, consistency, and compliance with regulatory standards. The results indicate that aligning governance practices with organizational objectives enhances overall business performance, with improvement in business outcomes emerging as the strongest predictor of governance effectiveness. Additionally, decision-making enhancement and post-governance quality improvements contribute to optimizing data management processes. Despite some industry-specific variations, the study reinforces the importance of structured governance frameworks in fostering operational efficiency and strategic alignment.

While the research provides valuable empirical insights, certain limitations, such as response bias and the study's cross-sectional nature, suggest that further exploration is needed. Future studies could adopt longitudinal approaches to track governance impacts over time and explore sector-specific challenges in industries with lower governance adoption rates. Nonetheless, this study offers a strong foundation for organizations seeking to refine their governance models, providing actionable recommendations for enhancing data management practices. Large organisations can strengthen their data governance strategies by prioritizing governance frameworks that align with business goals and leveraging emerging technologies, ensuring sustainable growth, compliance, and informed decision-making in an increasingly data-driven environment.

CHAPTER IV:
RESULTS

4.1 Introduction

The graphs generated in this chapter provide a visual representation of key findings related to the impact of data governance frameworks on data quality, business outcomes, and decision-making processes. These graphs illustrate patterns, trends, and relationships between governance practices and organizational performance, allowing for a more straightforward interpretation of complex statistical results. Various graphs, including bar charts, scatter plots, and correlation matrices, depict demographic distributions, response patterns, and statistical associations between variables. For example, regression analysis results are visualized to show the strength and direction of relationships between governance effectiveness and business success metrics. Correlation heat-maps highlight the degree of association between different governance components, helping to identify key success factors. These visualizations enhance the understanding of quantitative data by making statistical insights more accessible and interpretable, enabling organizations to make informed decisions about optimizing their data governance strategies.

4.2 Demographic Information

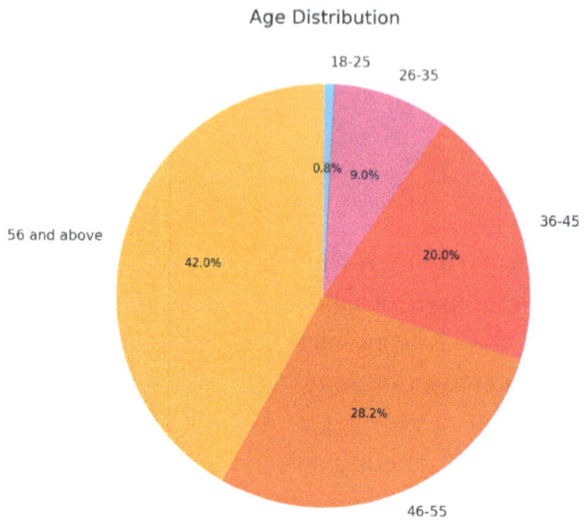

Figure 1. Age Distribution

The total number of participants in the survey is 255. The age distribution shows that the largest group of respondents, 42.0% (107 participants), falls within the 56 and above age category. This is followed by the 46-55 age group, which accounts for 28.2% (72 participants). The 36-45 age group represents 20.0% (51 participants), while the 26-35 age group contributes 9.0% (23 participants). The smallest representation comes from the 18-25 age group, comprising only 0.8% (2 participants).

Interpretation:

The majority of survey participants belong to the 46 years and above categories, with the 56 and above group being the most dominant. This suggests that the survey content likely appealed more to senior professionals with substantial career experience. In contrast, younger age groups (18-25 and 26-35) are underrepresented, collectively making up less than 10% of the total participants, indicating a limited connection or relevance of the survey topic to early-career individuals. The 36-45 age group, representing mid-career professionals, contributed a moderate portion to the participant pool. The age distribution indicates that the survey findings are primarily reflective of insights from experienced and senior professionals, which could influence the outcomes depending on the focus of the survey. For broader applicability, future surveys may need to target younger participants to ensure a more balanced age representation.

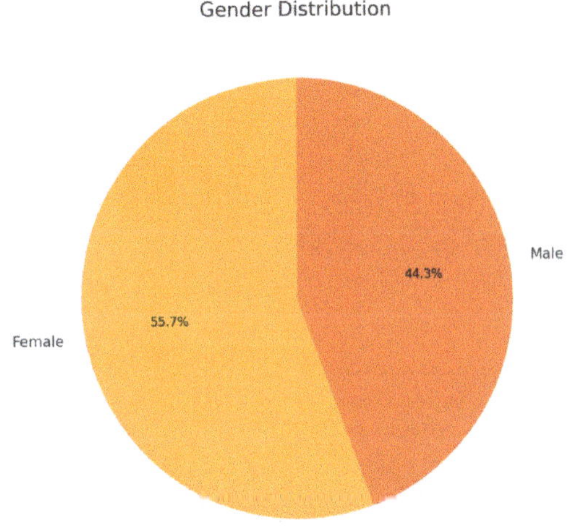

Figure 2. Gender Distribution

The gender distribution indicates that **55.7%** of the participants (142 participants) are female, while **44.3%** (113 participants) are male. This reflects a higher representation of female participants compared to males in the survey.

Interpretation:

The gender distribution reveals a slightly higher engagement from female participants, with 142 females compared to 113 males. This suggests that the topic might resonate more with women or that they were more accessible during the data collection process. The nearly balanced representation ensures a diverse range of perspectives, which can enhance the inclusiveness and reliability of the survey findings.

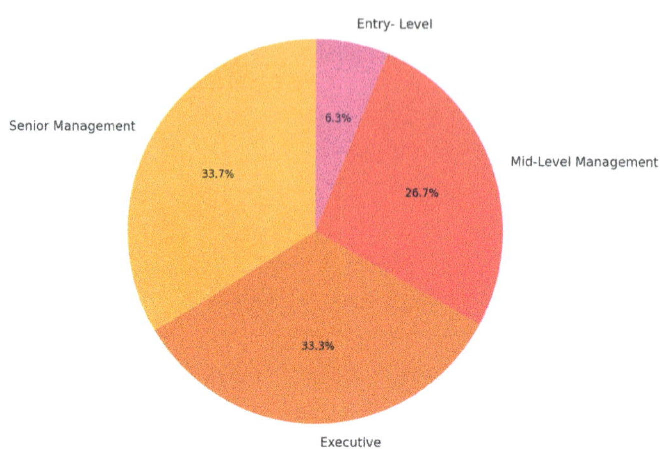

Figure 3. Position Distribution

The position distribution among participants reveals that **33.7%** (86 participants) are from Senior Management, making it the largest group represented in the survey. This is closely followed by participants in Executive roles, who account for **33.3%** (85 participants). Mid-Level Management constitutes **26.7%** (68 participants), indicating a substantial level of participation from this category as well. Meanwhile, Entry-Level positions are the least represented, comprising only **6.3%** (16 participants) of the total respondents.

Interpretation:

The data indicates that the majority of survey participants are in higher organizational roles, with Senior Management and Executives collectively representing **67.0%** (171 participants) of the total respondents. This significant representation from individuals in strategic leadership roles suggests that the survey topic is highly relevant to those with decision-making responsibilities or influence over organizational policies.

Mid-Level Management, accounting for **26.7%**, also demonstrates considerable engagement, which could reflect the involvement of this group in operationalizing or managing policies relevant to the survey. The relatively low representation from Entry-Level positions, at just **6.3%**, indicates limited engagement from individuals at the early stages of their careers. This may point to a lack of perceived relevance of the survey topic to this group or limited accessibility to such roles during data collection.

The strong presence of higher-level roles in the data ensures that the insights and findings of the survey will primarily reflect the perspectives of experienced professionals with significant organizational influence. However, the underrepresentation of Entry-Level employees may mean that the challenges and views of this group are less likely to be captured, which could impact the inclusivity of the findings. Future surveys could consider strategies to balance representation across all organizational levels for a more comprehensive perspective.

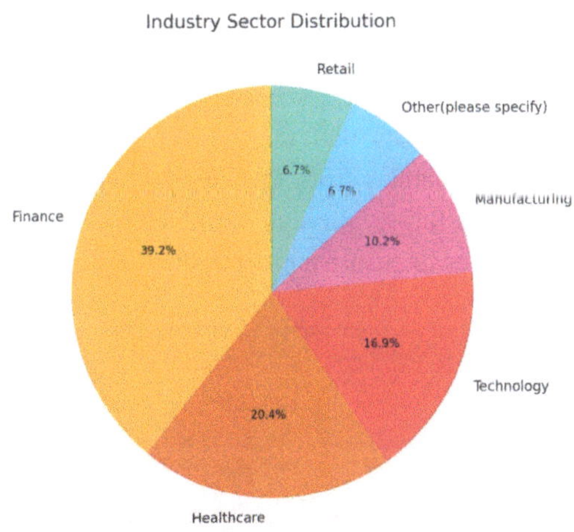

Figure 4. Industry Sector Distribution

The industry sector distribution reveals that the **Finance** sector has the largest representation, with **39.2%** (100 participants). This is followed by the **Healthcare** sector, which accounts for **20.4%** (52 participants). The **Technology** sector represents **16.9%** (43 participants), while **Manufacturing** contributes **10.2%** (26 participants). Both **Retail** and **Other (please specify)** categories have equal representation, each constituting **6.7%** (17 participants).

Interpretation:

The survey data shows a dominant representation from the Finance sector, comprising nearly 40% of the participants. This significant presence could indicate a strong interest or relevance of the survey topic to the Finance industry, where data governance, analytics, or related frameworks might play a critical role. The Healthcare sector, which represents just over 20%, also shows substantial engagement, likely reflecting the sector's growing emphasis on data management due to regulatory and operational demands.

The Technology sector, while slightly lower at 16.9%, indicates notable participation, aligning with its role as a key driver of innovation in data governance and related practices. Manufacturing, Retail, and Other sectors are less represented, suggesting either lower relevance of the topic to these industries or challenges in engaging participants from these sectors.

This distribution suggests that the survey findings will predominantly reflect perspectives and practices from the Finance and Healthcare sectors. To achieve broader insights, future surveys could consider targeted outreach to underrepresented industries to ensure a more balanced and inclusive perspective.

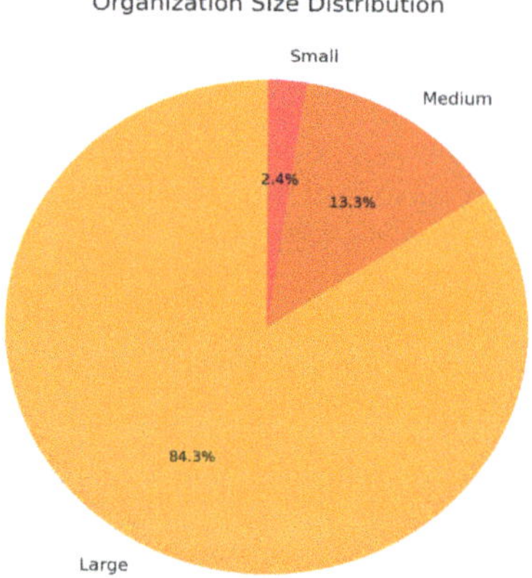

The organization size distribution indicates that **84.3%** of the respondents (215 participants) are from large organizations. Medium-sized organizations account for **13.3%** (34 participants), while small organizations make up only **2.4%** (6 participants).

Interpretation:

The overwhelming representation from large organizations, accounting for over four-fifths of the respondents, suggests that the survey topic resonates strongly with or is more relevant to larger entities. This could be due to the greater emphasis on structured frameworks, such as data governance, in larger organizations, which often handle vast and complex datasets requiring robust systems.

The medium-sized organizations, contributing 13.3%, show some engagement, possibly reflecting their growing adoption of structured frameworks as they scale operations. The small organizations, with a minimal representation of just 2.4%, may indicate limited relevance of the survey topic to their operational scale or potential challenges in engaging participants from this category.

Overall, the findings are likely to predominantly reflect the perspectives, challenges, and practices of large organizations. For future surveys aiming for broader applicability, targeted outreach to medium and small organizations may be necessary to capture a more balanced view.

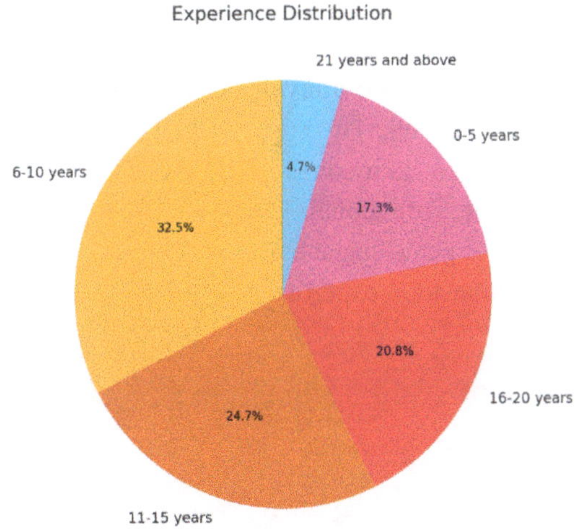

Figure 5 Experience Distribution

The experience distribution reveals that the largest group of respondents has **6-10 years** of experience, comprising **32.5%** (83 participants). The second-largest group is those with **11-15 years** of experience, accounting for **24.7%** (63 participants). Participants with **16-20 years** of experience represent **20.8%** (53 participants). The **0-5 years** group makes up **17.3%** (44 participants), while the least represented group, those with **21 years and above** of experience, constitutes only **4.7%** (12 participants).

Interpretation:

The distribution of experience suggests a diverse range of professional backgrounds, with a dominant presence of participants from the **6-10 years** and **11-15 years** categories, together accounting for **57.2%** (146 participants) of the total responses. This suggests that the survey attracted professionals with moderate to substantial experience, likely those in mid-career stages who are shaping or influencing organizational practices.

The **16-20 years** group also contributes a significant portion, which could indicate the involvement of seasoned professionals who are likely in senior roles or leadership positions. The **0-5 years** group, with **17.3%**, reflects a solid representation of newer entrants to the workforce, indicating that the survey's topic may also appeal to early-career professionals.

However, the **21 years and above** group, at just **4.7%**, represents a very small portion of the respondents. This suggests that the survey may not have had strong representation from individuals with extensive experience, possibly excluding the most senior professionals in the field. For future surveys, it may be beneficial to ensure stronger engagement with this group to gain perspectives from individuals with long-term expertise.

4.3 Impact of Data Governance on Data Quality & Business Outcome

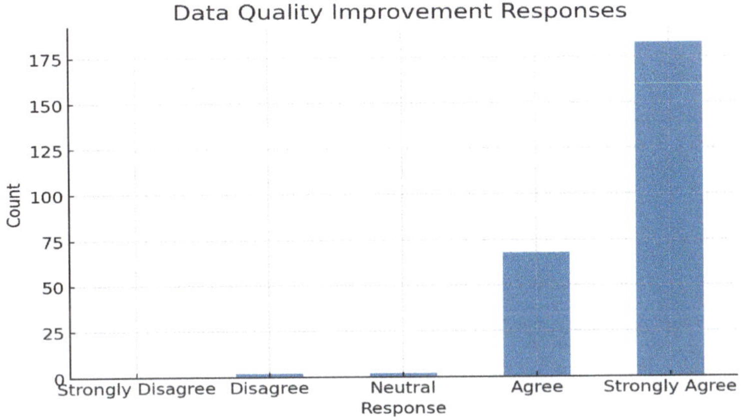

Figure 6. Data Quality Improvement Responses

A significant majority of participants, 183 individuals (71.8%), strongly agree that data governance frameworks lead to substantial improvements in data quality. Another 68 participants (26.7%) agree with this assertion, reflecting strong overall support. Only 2 participants (0.8%) are neutral, and another 2 participants (0.8%) disagree. No participants strongly disagreed, indicating an overwhelmingly positive sentiment toward the impact of data governance frameworks on data quality.

Interpretation:

The data demonstrates a clear consensus among respondents about the benefits of data governance in improving data quality, with 98.5% either agreeing or strongly agreeing. The negligible neutral and disagreement responses suggest that doubts about the effectiveness of governance frameworks are rare. This strong agreement highlights the importance of adopting and refining governance practices to enhance organizational data quality and foster trust in data-driven decision-making.

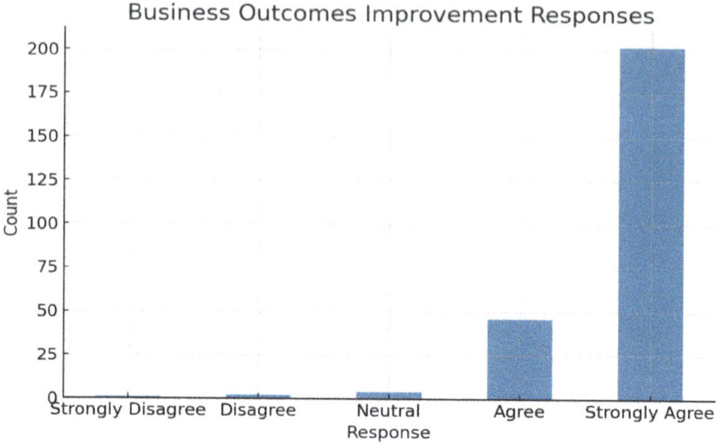

Figure 7 Business Outcomes Improvement Responses

The majority of participants, 202 individuals (79.2%), strongly agree that data governance frameworks improve business outcomes. An additional 46 participants (18.0%) agree, showing significant overall support. A small number of participants remain neutral, with 4 individuals (1.6%), while 2 participants (0.8%) disagree and 1 participant (0.4%) strongly disagrees.

Interpretation:

The responses indicate an overwhelming positive consensus, with 97.2% of participants either agreeing or strongly agreeing that data governance frameworks contribute to improved business outcomes. The minimal neutral and disagreement responses reflect a shared recognition of the value data governance provides in enhancing organizational performance. These findings emphasize the importance of integrating governance practices as a strategy for achieving better business results.

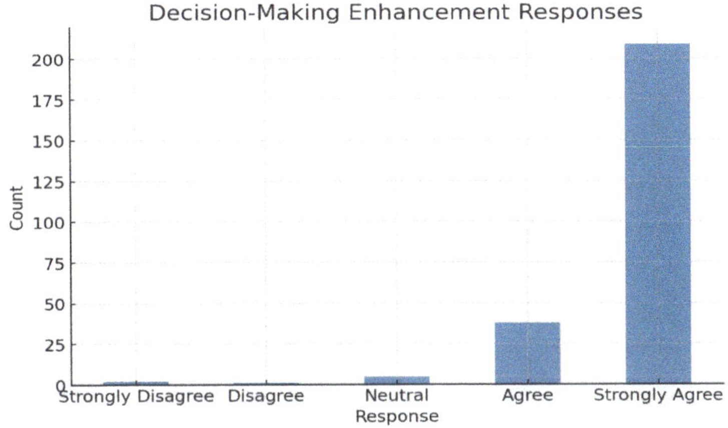

Figure 8. Decision Making Enhancement Responses

For the question on whether data governance frameworks enhance decision-making, the majority of participants, 209 individuals (82.0%), strongly agree. Another 38 participants (14.9%) agree, contributing to a significant overall agreement. A small group, comprising 5 participants (2.0%), is neutral, indicating some uncertainty. Only 1 participant (0.4%) disagrees, while 2 participants (0.8%) strongly disagree, reflecting minimal opposition to the assertion.

Interpretation:

The responses indicate an overwhelmingly positive sentiment regarding the role of data governance in enhancing decision-making processes, with 96.9% of participants either agreeing or strongly agreeing. This strong agreement highlights the perceived effectiveness of governance frameworks in providing reliable, accurate, and actionable data to support critical decisions. The minimal neutral and disagreement responses suggest that only a small fraction of participants have reservations, possibly due to specific organizational challenges or varying levels of implementation maturity.

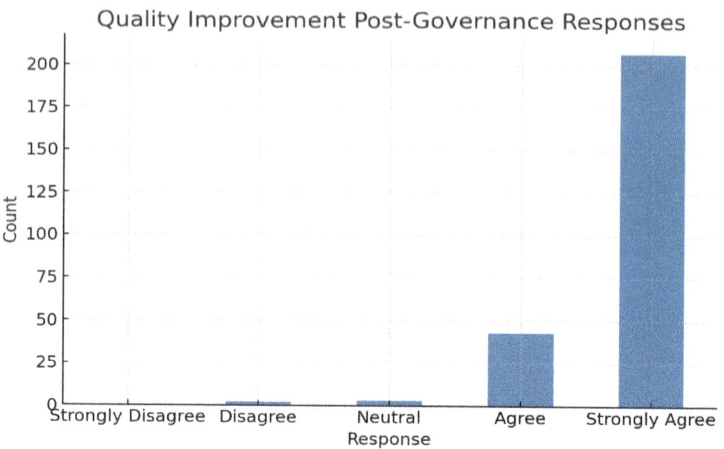

Figure 9. Quality Improvement Post-Governance Responses

For the question on quality improvement post-governance, the majority of participants, 207 individuals (81.2%), strongly agree that data governance frameworks significantly enhance data quality. An additional 43 participants (16.9%) agree, making up a substantial portion of the responses. Only 3 participants (1.2%) remain neutral, indicating minimal uncertainty, while 2 participants (0.8%) disagree. No participants strongly disagreed with the statement.

Interpretation:

The results demonstrate a strong consensus among respondents about the positive impact of data governance frameworks on improving data quality after their implementation. With 98.1% of participants agreeing or strongly agreeing, the data underscores the effectiveness of governance practices in ensuring quality improvements. The negligible neutral and disagreement responses suggest widespread recognition of these benefits across diverse organizational contexts.

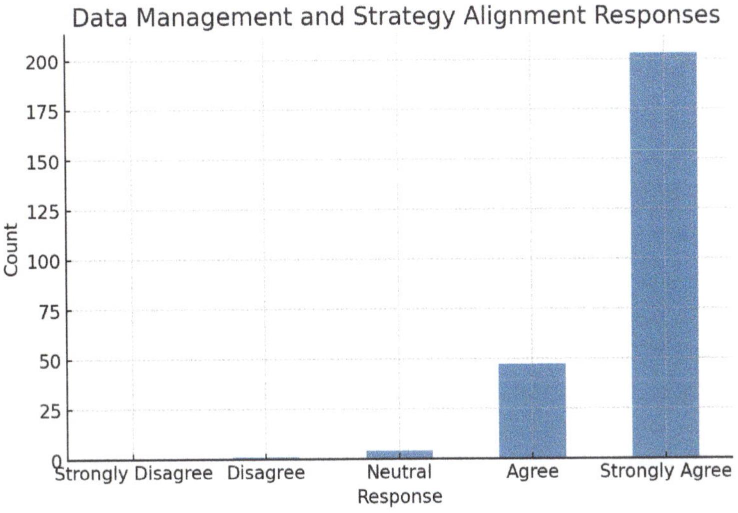

Figure 10. Data Management & Strategy Alignment Responses

The majority of participants, 203 individuals (79.6%), strongly agree that data governance frameworks effectively align data management practices with organizational strategies. Another 47 participants (18.4%) agree with this statement, demonstrating strong overall support. A small fraction, 4 participants (1.6%), remain neutral, while only 1 participant (0.4%) disagrees. No participants strongly disagreed with the statement.

Interpretation:

The responses reveal a clear consensus that data governance frameworks play a pivotal role in aligning data management practices with organizational strategies. With 98% of participants either agreeing or strongly agreeing, it is evident that data governance is perceived as a critical enabler of strategic alignment. The minimal neutral and disagreement responses suggest that participants broadly recognize the importance of governance in ensuring that data management initiatives support overarching business objectives.

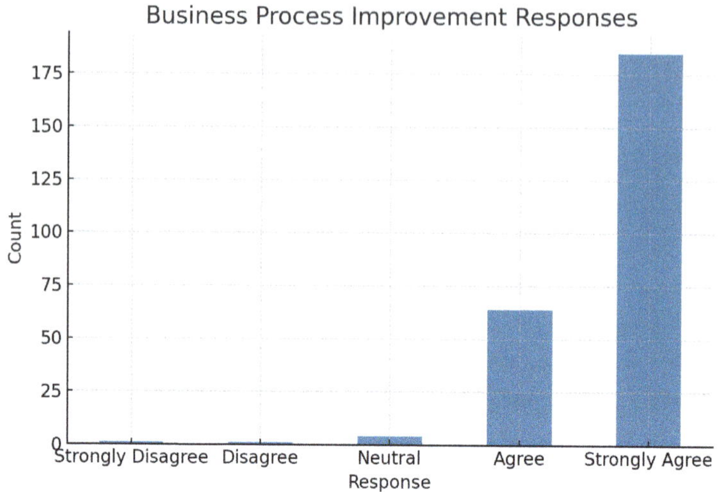

Figure 11. Business Process Improvement Responses

For the question on whether data governance frameworks improve business processes, 185 participants (72.5%) strongly agree, while 64 participants (25.1%) agree, reflecting strong overall support. A small group of 4 participants (1.6%) remains neutral, indicating minor uncertainty. Only 1 participant each (0.4%) disagrees or strongly disagrees, showing negligible opposition.

Interpretation:

The responses reveal a significant consensus that data governance frameworks play a vital role in enhancing business process efficiency and effectiveness, with 97.6% of participants either agreeing or strongly agreeing. The minimal neutral and disagreement responses suggest that any doubts about this impact are rare and may be due to unique organizational challenges or the maturity of governance practices.

Test 1: Regression Analysis

```
Regression Analysis with 'Data Quality Improvement' as the dependent
variable:
                              OLS Regression Results
======================================================================
=============
Dep. Variable:     Data Quality Improvement   R-squared:
0.378
Model:                                  OLS   Adj. R-squared:
0.365
Method:                       Least Squares   F-statistic:
30.25
Date:                      Fri, 20 Dec 2024   Prob (F-statistic):
5.44e-24
Time:                              08:39:19   Log-Likelihood:
-136.74
No. Observations:                       255   AIC:
285.5
Df Residuals:                           249   BIC:
306.7
Df Model:                                 5
Covariance Type:                  nonrobust
======================================================================
==================================
                                              coef    std err          t
P>|t|      [0.025      0.975]
----------------------------------------------------------------------
----------------------------------
const                                       1.2728      0.312      4.076
0.000       0.658       1.888
Business Outcomes Improvement               0.3680      0.067      5.466
0.000       0.235       0.501
Decision-Making Enhancement                 0.0583      0.064      0.918
0.360      -0.067       0.183
Quality Improvement Post-Governance         0.0526      0.069      0.759
0.448      -0.084       0.189
Data Management and Strategy Alignment      0.1581      0.069      2.298
0.022       0.023       0.294
Business Process Improvement                0.0830      0.060      1.386
0.167      -0.035       0.201
======================================================================
=======
Omnibus:                      40.956   Durbin-Watson:
1.955
Prob(Omnibus):                 0.000   Jarque-Bera (JB):
55.847
Skew:                         -1.051   Prob(JB):
7.47e-13
Kurtosis:                      3.915   Cond. No.
128.
======================================================================
=======

Notes:
[1] Standard Errors assume that the covariance matrix of the errors is
correctly specified.
```

```
Regression Analysis with 'Business Outcomes Improvement' as the
dependent variable:
                                  OLS Regression Results
==============================================================================
==================
Dep. Variable:     Business Outcomes Improvement   R-squared:
0.568
Model:                                       OLS   Adj. R-squared:
0.560
Method:                            Least Squares   F-statistic:
65.54
Date:                           Fri, 20 Dec 2024   Prob (F-statistic):
1.77e-43
Time:                                   08:39:19   Log-Likelihood:
-106.84
No. Observations:                            255   AIC:
225.7
Df Residuals:                                249   BIC:
246.9
Df Model:                                      5
Covariance Type:                       nonrobust
==============================================================================
====================================
                                             coef    std err          t
P>|t|      [0.025      0.975]
------------------------------------------------------------------------------
------------------------------------
const                                     -0.0751      0.287     -0.262
0.794      -0.640       0.490
Data Quality Improvement                   0.2911      0.053      5.466
0.000       0.186       0.396
Decision-Making Enhancement                0.3318      0.053      6.316
0.000       0.228       0.435
Quality Improvement Post-Governance        0.1382      0.061      2.265
0.024       0.018       0.258
Data Management and Strategy Alignment     0.1092      0.061      1.777
0.077      -0.012       0.230
Business Process Improvement               0.1478      0.053      2.807
0.005       0.044       0.251
==============================================================================
=======
Omnibus:                       52.946   Durbin-Watson:
2.290
Prob(Omnibus):                  0.000   Jarque-Bera (JB):
117.725
Skew:                          -0.997   Prob(JB):
2.73e-26
Kurtosis:                       5.666   Cond. No.
132.
==============================================================================
=======

Notes:
[1] Standard Errors assume that the covariance matrix of the errors is
correctly specified.

Regression Analysis with 'Decision-Making Enhancement' as the dependent
variable:
                                 OLS Regression Results
```

```
==============================================================================
================
Dep. Variable:      Decision-Making Enhancement   R-squared:
0.493
Model:                                     OLS   Adj. R-squared:
0.483
Method:                          Least Squares   F-statistic:
48.38
Date:                         Fri, 20 Dec 2024   Prob (F-statistic):
7.36e-35
Time:                                 08:39:19   Log-Likelihood:
-135.73
No. Observations:                          255   AIC:
283.5
Df Residuals:                              249   BIC:
304.7
Df Model:                                    5
Covariance Type:                     nonrobust
==============================================================================
===================================
                                                coef    std err          t
P>|t|      [0.025      0.975]
------------------------------------------------------------------------------
-----------------------------------
const                                         0.2809      0.321      0.876
0.382      -0.351       0.913
Data Quality Improvement                      0.0578      0.063      0.918
0.360      -0.066       0.182
Business Outcomes Improvement                 0.4162      0.066      6.316
0.000       0.286       0.546
Quality Improvement Post-Governance           0.3031      0.066      4.572
0.000       0.173       0.434
Data Management and Strategy Alignment        0.1136      0.069      1.650
0.100      -0.022       0.249
Business Process Improvement                  0.0527      0.060      0.881
0.379      -0.065       0.170
==============================================================================
=======
Omnibus:                      150.091   Durbin-Watson:
1.753
Prob(Omnibus):                  0.000   Jarque-Bera (JB):
1713.319
Skew:                          -2.104   Prob(JB):
0.00
Kurtosis:                      14.981   Cond. No.
132.
==============================================================================
=======

Notes:
[1] Standard Errors assume that the covariance matrix of the errors is
correctly specified.

Regression Analysis with 'Quality Improvement Post-Governance' as the
dependent variable:
                                     OLS Regression Results
==============================================================================
========================
Dep. Variable:      Quality Improvement Post-Governance   R-squared:
0.403
```

```
Model:                                               OLS   Adj. R-
squared:                0.391
Method:                                    Least Squares   F-statistic:
33.66
Date:                                   Fri, 20 Dec 2024   Prob (F-
statistic):         3.34e-26
Time:                                           08:39:19   Log-
Likelihood:                  -113.91
No. Observations:                                    255   AIC:
239.8
Df Residuals:                                        249   BIC:
261.1
Df Model:                                              5
Covariance Type:                               nonrobust
=========================================================================
===================================
                                              coef    std err          t
P>|t|      [0.025      0.975]
-------------------------------------------------------------------------
-----------------------------------
const                                       1.4447      0.280      5.154
0.000       0.893       1.997
Data Quality Improvement                    0.0439      0.058      0.759
0.448      -0.070       0.158
Business Outcomes Improvement               0.1461      0.064      2.265
0.024       0.019       0.273
Decision-Making Enhancement                 0.2555      0.056      4.572
0.000       0.145       0.366
Data Management and Strategy Alignment      0.1134      0.063      1.795
0.074      -0.011       0.238
Business Process Improvement                0.1450      0.054      2.676
0.008       0.038       0.252
=========================================================================
=======
Omnibus:                       56.057   Durbin-Watson:
1.669
Prob(Omnibus):                  0.000   Jarque-Bera (JB):
90.538
Skew:                          -1.246   Prob(JB):
2.19e-20
Kurtosis:                       4.521   Cond. No.
126.
=========================================================================
=======

Notes:
[1] Standard Errors assume that the covariance matrix of the errors is
correctly specified.

Regression Analysis with 'Data Management and Strategy Alignment' as
the dependent variable:
                                 OLS Regression Results
=========================================================================
==========================
Dep. Variable:     Data Management and Strategy Alignment   R-squared:
0.384
Model:                                               OLS   Adj. R-
squared:                0.371
Method:                                    Least Squares   F-
statistic:                   31.01
```

```
Date:                                     Fri, 20 Dec 2024   Prob (F-
statistic):            1.73e-24
Time:                                             08:39:19   Log-
Likelihood:                 -113.07
No. Observations:                                      255   AIC:
238.1
Df Residuals:                                          249   BIC:
259.4
Df Model:                                                5
Covariance Type:                                 nonrobust
==============================================================================
================================
                                         coef    std err          t
P>|t|      [0.025      0.975]
------------------------------------------------------------------------------
--------------------------------
const                                  1.4707      0.279      5.276
0.000       0.922       2.020
Data Quality Improvement               0.1313      0.057      2.298
0.022       0.019       0.244
Business Outcomes Improvement          0.1147      0.065      1.777
0.077      -0.012       0.242
Decision-Making Enhancement            0.0951      0.058      1.650
0.100      -0.018       0.209
Quality Improvement Post-Governance    0.1126      0.063      1.795
0.074      -0.011       0.236
Business Process Improvement           0.2448      0.053      4.658
0.000       0.141       0.348
==============================================================================
=======
Omnibus:                       54.469   Durbin-Watson:
1.954
Prob(Omnibus):                  0.000   Jarque-Bera (JB):
88.721
Skew:                          -1.198   Prob(JB):
5.43e-20
Kurtosis:                       4.614   Cond. No.
125.
==============================================================================
=======

Notes:
[1] Standard Errors assume that the covariance matrix of the errors is
correctly specified.

Regression Analysis with 'Business Process Improvement' as the
dependent variable:
                                 OLS Regression Results
==============================================================================
=================
Dep. Variable:     Business Process Improvement   R-squared:
0.398
Model:                                      OLS   Adj. R-squared:
0.386
Method:                           Least Squares   F-statistic:
32.94
Date:                          Fri, 20 Dec 2024   Prob (F-statistic):
9.61e-26
Time:                                  08:39:19   Log-Likelihood:
-150.13
```

```
No. Observations:                           255   AIC:
312.3
Df Residuals:                               249   BIC:
333.5
Df Model:                                     5
Covariance Type:                      nonrobust
=========================================================================
===================================
                                         coef    std err          t
P>|t|      [0.025      0.975]
-------------------------------------------------------------------------
-----------------------------------
const                                  0.5063      0.338      1.496
0.136      -0.160       1.173
Data Quality Improvement               0.0922      0.067      1.386
0.167      -0.039       0.223
Business Outcomes Improvement          0.2075      0.074      2.807
0.005       0.062       0.353
Decision-Making Enhancement            0.0590      0.067      0.881
0.379      -0.073       0.191
Quality Improvement Post-Governance    0.1927      0.072      2.676
0.008       0.051       0.335
Data Management and Strategy Alignment 0.3274      0.070      4.658
0.000       0.189       0.466
=========================================================================
=======
Omnibus:                     71.699   Durbin-Watson:
2.021
Prob(Omnibus):                0.000   Jarque-Bera (JB):
157.422
Skew:                        -1.360   Prob(JB):
6.55e-35
Kurtosis:                     5.724   Cond. No.
132.
=========================================================================
=======

Notes:

[1] Standard Errors assume that the covariance matrix of the errors is
correctly specified.
```

Observations and Interpretation:

1. Data Quality Improvement:

Key Insights:

Business Outcomes Improvement has a **strong and positive influence** on Data Quality Improvement ($p < 0.001$), suggesting that better business outcomes are closely tied to enhanced data quality.

Data Management and Strategy Alignment also has a **statistically significant impact** ($p = 0.022$), indicating that aligning data management practices with business goals directly improves data quality.

Other factors like Decision-Making Enhancement and Quality Improvement Post-Governance were not statistically significant, meaning their effect on data quality is limited or inconsistent.

Interpretation: This model highlights that **strategic alignment and measurable business outcomes** are the primary drivers of improved data quality in large organizations. Focusing on these areas can yield tangible improvements in data governance efforts.

2. Business Outcomes Improvement:

Key Insights:

Decision-Making Enhancement ($p < 0.001$) and Data Quality Improvement ($p < 0.001$) have the **strongest positive effects**, showing that both better decisions and high-quality data are critical for achieving improved business outcomes.

Quality Improvement Post-Governance ($p = 0.024$) and Business Process Improvement ($p = 0.005$) also significantly influence business outcomes but to a lesser extent.

Interpretation: The results emphasize that **effective decision-making and high-quality data** form the backbone of improved business outcomes. Organizations should prioritize governance frameworks that enable data-driven decisions and focus on governance initiatives that enhance data quality and processes.

3. Decision-Making Enhancement:

Key Insights:

Business Outcomes Improvement ($p < 0.001$) and Quality Improvement Post-Governance ($p < 0.001$) significantly impact Decision-Making Enhancement, indicating a **strong relationship between better outcomes, improved governance, and decision-making capabilities**.

Other factors such as Data Management and Strategy Alignment and Business Process Improvement were less influential.

Interpretation: This analysis underscores the importance of **clear governance frameworks** and **outcome-focused strategies** in fostering decision-making capabilities. Organizations that achieve measurable outcomes and better governance are more likely to empower effective decision-making.

4. Quality Improvement Post-Governance:

Key Insights:

Both Decision-Making Enhancement ($p < 0.001$) and Business Outcomes Improvement ($p = 0.024$) play critical roles in driving improvements in data quality after implementing governance frameworks.

Business Process Improvement ($p = 0.008$) also positively affects Quality Improvement Post-Governance.

Interpretation: This finding highlights the **cascading benefits** of effective governance frameworks. As organizations improve decision-making and business outcomes, they see noticeable enhancements in data quality, validating the value of structured governance practices.

5. Business Process Improvement:

Key Insights:

Data Management and Strategy Alignment ($p < 0.001$) emerged as the most significant predictor, demonstrating that aligning governance practices with strategic goals directly enhances business processes.

Business Outcomes Improvement ($p = 0.005$) and Quality Improvement Post-Governance ($p = 0.008$) also play significant roles.

Interpretation: This analysis reaffirms the **centrality of alignment between data strategies and business objectives**. Effective governance frameworks drive business process improvements by ensuring strategic coherence and focusing on measurable outcomes

Overall Conclusion:

Across all analyses, two factors consistently emerged as significant:

Strategic Alignment: Aligning data management practices with business objectives is pivotal for enhancing data quality, decision-making, and business processes.

Outcome-Focused Governance: Frameworks that prioritize measurable business outcomes significantly impact overall governance effectiveness.

Organizations should focus on **integrating governance frameworks with strategic business goals and enhancing decision-making processes** to achieve sustained improvements in data quality and operational efficiency.

Objective 1: Test 2: Correlation Analysis

```
Correlation Matrix:
                                          Data Quality Improvement  \
Data Quality Improvement                                  1.000000
Business Outcomes Improvement                             0.579915
Decision-Making Enhancement                               0.451750
Quality Improvement Post-Governance                       0.399734
Data Management and Strategy Alignment                    0.439997
Business Process Improvement                              0.423600

                                          Business Outcomes Improvement  \
Data Quality Improvement                                       0.579915
Business Outcomes Improvement                                  1.000000
Decision-Making Enhancement                                    0.643982
Quality Improvement Post-Governance                            0.532071
Data Management and Strategy Alignment                         0.502355
Business Process Improvement                                   0.525640

                                          Decision-Making Enhancement  \
Data Quality Improvement                                     0.451750
Business Outcomes Improvement                                0.643982
Decision-Making Enhancement                                  1.000000
Quality Improvement Post-Governance                          0.557543
Data Management and Strategy Alignment                       0.459875
Business Process Improvement                                 0.455013

                                          Quality Improvement Post-
Governance  \
Data Quality Improvement
0.399734
Business Outcomes Improvement
0.532071
Decision-Making Enhancement
0.557543
Quality Improvement Post-Governance
1.000000
Data Management and Strategy Alignment
0.441789
Business Process Improvement
0.469762

                                          Data Management and Strategy
Alignment  \
Data Quality Improvement
0.439997
Business Outcomes Improvement
0.502355
Decision-Making Enhancement
0.459875
Quality Improvement Post-Governance
0.441789
Data Management and Strategy Alignment
1.000000
Business Process Improvement
0.523596

                                          Business Process Improvement
Data Quality Improvement                                      0.423600
```

```
Business Outcomes Improvement                         0.525640
Decision-Making Enhancement                           0.455013
Quality Improvement Post-Governance                   0.469762
Data Management and Strategy Alignment                0.523596

Business Process Improvement                          1.000000
```

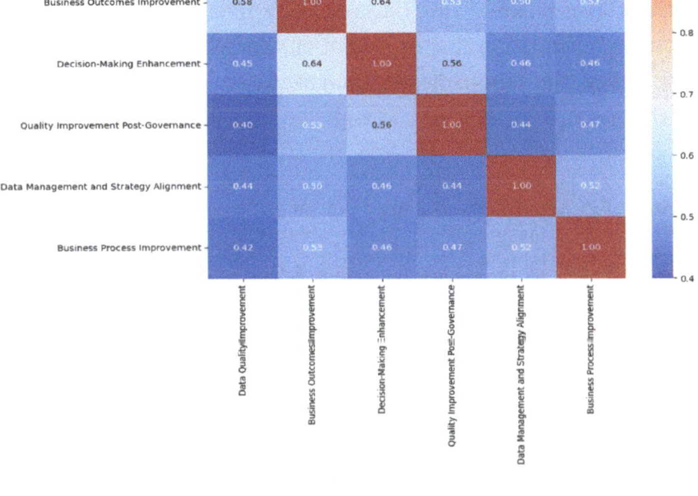

Figure 12. Correlation Heatmap (Objective 1)

Observations and Interpretation:

1. Strong Relationship Between Business Outcomes and Data Quality

Observation: The correlation between Business Outcomes Improvement and Data Quality Improvement is **strong** (r = 0.579). Similarly, Decision-Making Enhancement and Business Outcomes Improvement exhibit a high correlation (r = 0.644).

Interpretation: This indicates that **better business outcomes drive significant improvements in data quality** and decision-making. When organizations focus on achieving measurable business outcomes, they naturally enhance the quality of their data and decision-making processes. This aligns with the research's emphasis on the **strategic role of governance in improving organizational performance**.

2. Moderate Impact of Post-Governance Efforts

Observation: Quality Improvement Post-Governance has moderate correlations with Decision-Making Enhancement (r = 0.558) and Business Outcomes Improvement (r = 0.532).

Interpretation: This highlights the **importance of continued efforts after implementing governance frameworks**. Sustained governance practices lead to improved decision-making and business outcomes. This finding echoes the research's recommendation that organizations **focus on long-term governance strategies rather than one-time implementations**.

3. Strategic Alignment as a Key Factor

Observation: Data Management and Strategy Alignment shows moderate correlations with Business Outcomes Improvement (r = 0.502) and Business Process Improvement (r = 0.524).

Interpretation: Aligning data governance practices with organizational goals is **critical for enhancing business processes and outcomes**. This validates the research objective of identifying alignment as a **core success factor for effective governance frameworks**.

4. Weaker Influence of Individual Factors on Data Quality

Observation: Factors like Quality Improvement Post-Governance and Business Process Improvement show weaker correlations with Data Quality Improvement (r = 0.400 and r = 0.424, respectively).

Interpretation: While these factors contribute to governance effectiveness, their **direct impact on data quality is limited**. This suggests that organizations should focus on **holistic strategies that encompass multiple dimensions of governance**.

Key Takeaways:

Focus on Business Outcomes: The strong relationship between business outcomes and other governance elements underlines its pivotal role. Achieving business success directly supports data quality, decision-making, and governance impact.

Prioritize Long-Term Governance: Moderate correlations for post-governance improvements indicate that organizations should maintain ongoing efforts to enhance decision-making and business processes.

Ensure Strategic Alignment: Governance frameworks must align with business strategies to maximize their effectiveness and impact across the organization.

Conclusion:

This analysis emphasizes that **effective governance frameworks are interconnected systems**, where improvements in one area drive progress in others. Organizations must **prioritize strategic alignment, measurable outcomes, and long-term governance efforts** to achieve transformative impacts on data quality, decision-making, and business success.

Summary of Tests performed For Objective 1:

Regression Analysis:

The regression analysis for **Objective 1**—focused on factors driving data governance impacts—provides crucial insights into the relationships between key elements of governance frameworks.

1. Data Quality Improvement (Dependent Variable):

Business Outcomes Improvement emerged as the **strongest predictor**, with a significant positive influence. This reinforces the idea that measurable business success directly supports data quality.

Data Management and Strategy Alignment also had a meaningful impact, highlighting the importance of aligning governance practices with organizational goals.

Other factors, such as Decision-Making Enhancement and Quality Improvement Post-Governance, showed weaker or inconsistent effects.

Interpretation: Organizations seeking to improve data quality should focus on achieving tangible business outcomes and aligning governance strategies with broader organizational objectives.

2. Business Outcomes Improvement (Dependent Variable):

Decision-Making Enhancement and **Data Quality Improvement** were the **strongest contributors**, emphasizing that better decision-making and high-quality data significantly drive business success.

Business Process Improvement and Quality Improvement Post-Governance also had notable effects, but their impact was secondary.

Interpretation: Governance frameworks must prioritize effective decision-making processes and high-quality data to unlock business value and enhance outcomes.

3. Decision-Making Enhancement (Dependent Variable):

Business Outcomes Improvement and **Quality Improvement Post-Governance** had the most substantial effects, showing that measurable outcomes and governance efforts post-implementation significantly improve decision-making capabilities.

Other factors, such as Data Management and Strategy Alignment, had a limited direct impact.

Interpretation: Governance success in decision-making depends on achieving concrete business results and maintaining governance efforts even after initial implementation.

4. Quality Improvement Post-Governance (Dependent Variable):

Both **Decision-Making Enhancement** and **Business Outcomes Improvement** showed significant positive impacts, emphasizing the cascading benefits of effective governance.

Business Process Improvement also had a moderate influence, further underscoring the interconnected nature of governance elements.

Interpretation: Sustained efforts after governance implementation are critical to ensuring long-term improvements in data quality and processes.

5. Business Process Improvement (Dependent Variable):

Data Management and Strategy Alignment was the strongest factor, demonstrating the importance of integrating governance practices with strategic objectives.

Business Outcomes Improvement and Quality Improvement Post-Governance also contributed positively.

Interpretation: Aligning governance frameworks with organizational strategy is vital for driving improvements in business processes and operations.

Overall Insights:

Strategic Alignment Matters Most:

Aligning governance practices with organizational goals has the **strongest impact across multiple dimensions**, especially for business processes and data quality.

Post-Governance Efforts Are Key:

Maintaining governance efforts after initial implementation enhances decision-making, data quality, and processes over time.

Focus on Business Outcomes:

Achieving tangible business results is a **central driver** for governance success and positively influences decision-making, processes, and data quality.

Conclusion:

The analysis highlights that **effective governance frameworks rely on strategic alignment, measurable outcomes, and sustained efforts post-implementation**. By prioritizing these areas, organizations can maximize the value and impact of their governance initiatives.

Correlation Analysis:

The correlation analysis for **Objective 1**, which examines the interplay among governance elements, reveals key relationships and insights into how these factors drive governance success.

Key Findings:

Strong Relationships:

Business Outcomes Improvement shows a **strong positive correlation with Data Quality Improvement** (r = 0.580). This underscores that **achieving measurable business success directly enhances data quality**.

Decision-Making Enhancement is **highly correlated with Business Outcomes Improvement** (r = 0.644), emphasizing the role of effective decision-making in driving organizational success.

Moderate Relationships:

Quality Improvement Post-Governance has moderate correlations with both Decision-Making Enhancement (r = 0.558) and Business Outcomes Improvement (r = 0.532). This indicates that sustained governance efforts after implementation significantly influence decision-making and business outcomes.

Data Management and Strategy Alignment is moderately correlated with Business Outcomes Improvement (r = 0.502) and Business Process

Improvement (r = 0.524), highlighting the importance of aligning governance strategies with business objectives.

Weaker Relationships:

Data Quality Improvement has weaker correlations with Quality Improvement Post-Governance (r = 0.400) and Business Process Improvement (r = 0.424). This suggests that while related, their direct impact on data quality is less pronounced compared to other factors.

Interpretation:

Business Outcomes Drive Governance Success:

The strong correlation between Business Outcomes Improvement and other governance factors demonstrates its central role in ensuring governance effectiveness. By focusing on measurable outcomes, organizations can indirectly enhance data quality and decision-making.

Strategic Alignment is Essential:

The moderate correlations of Data Management and Strategy Alignment with multiple factors reaffirm its importance. **Aligning governance practices with organizational goals** ensures cohesive and impactful governance efforts.

Post-Governance Efforts Add Value:

Moderate relationships with Quality Improvement Post-Governance highlight the need for **sustained efforts after framework implementation**. These efforts improve decision-making capabilities and align governance with business strategies.

Holistic Approach Needed:

Weaker correlations for some factors suggest that **no single element alone can drive governance success**. A **comprehensive and integrated approach** is crucial for maximizing the impact of governance frameworks.

Conclusion:

The correlation analysis reveals that **business outcomes, strategic alignment, and post-governance efforts** are key drivers of governance success. Organizations must prioritize achieving measurable results, aligning governance with business objectives, and maintaining sustained efforts to unlock the full potential of their governance initiatives.

4.4 Key Success Factors for Data Governance Implementation

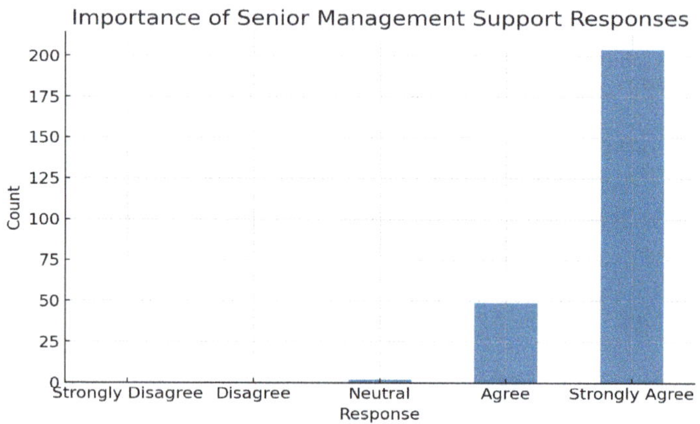

Figure 13. Importance of Senior Management Support Responses

The majority of participants, 204 individuals (80.0%), strongly agree that senior management support is critical for effective data governance. An additional 49 participants (19.2%) agree, collectively showing strong overall support. Only 2 participants (0.8%) remain neutral, while no participants disagreed or strongly disagreed.

Interpretation:

The responses highlight a unanimous consensus regarding the importance of senior management support in the success of data governance frameworks. With 99.2% of participants agreeing or strongly agreeing, it is clear that leadership buy-in is perceived as an essential factor for effective implementation. The negligible neutral responses emphasize that senior management's role is seen as indispensable in ensuring the success and sustainability of governance practices.

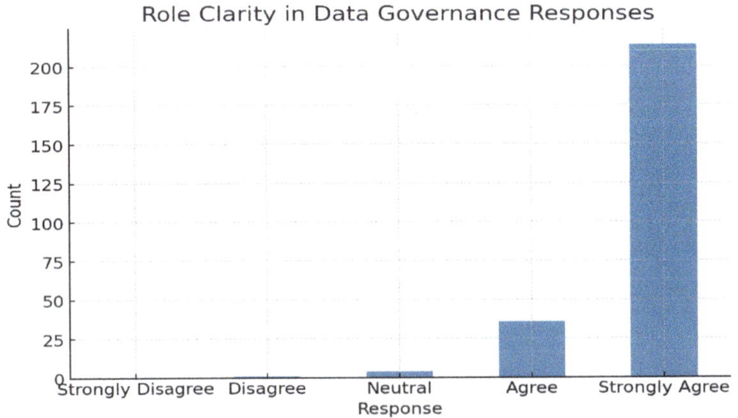

Figure 14. Role Clarity in Data Governance Responses

The majority of participants, 214 individuals (83.9%), strongly agree that role clarity is essential in data governance. Another 36 participants (14.1%) agree, collectively showing strong support. A small group of 4 participants (1.6%) remains neutral, while only 1 participant (0.4%) disagrees. No participants strongly disagreed with the statement.

Interpretation:

The responses reflect a strong consensus on the importance of clearly defined roles and responsibilities in the successful implementation of data governance frameworks. With 98% of participants agreeing or strongly agreeing, it is evident that role clarity is widely recognized as a critical factor for efficient governance. The minimal neutral and disagreement responses suggest that any uncertainty or opposition is rare, highlighting the consistent acknowledgment of this aspect's significance.

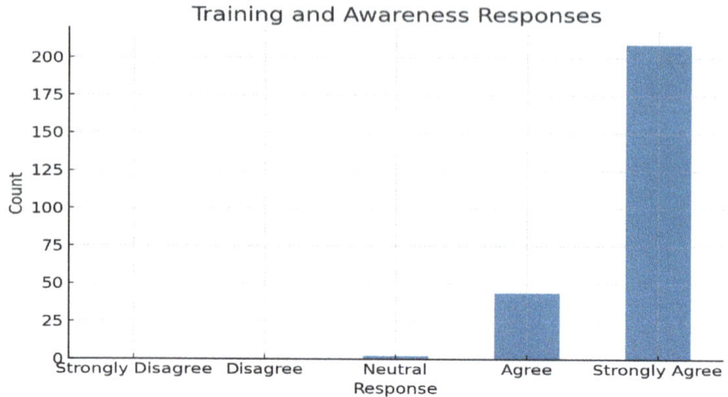

Figure 15. Training and Awareness Responses

The majority of participants, 209 individuals (82.0%), strongly agree that training and awareness are critical for effective data governance. Another 44 participants (17.3%) agree, collectively reflecting substantial support. Only 2 participants (0.8%) remain neutral, while no participants disagreed or strongly disagreed.

Interpretation:

The responses indicate a clear consensus on the importance of training and awareness in ensuring the success of data governance frameworks. With 99.3% of participants agreeing or strongly agreeing, it is evident that equipping employees with the necessary knowledge and skills is regarded as an essential factor for governance effectiveness. The negligible neutral responses suggest minimal uncertainty about this aspect, emphasizing its significance.

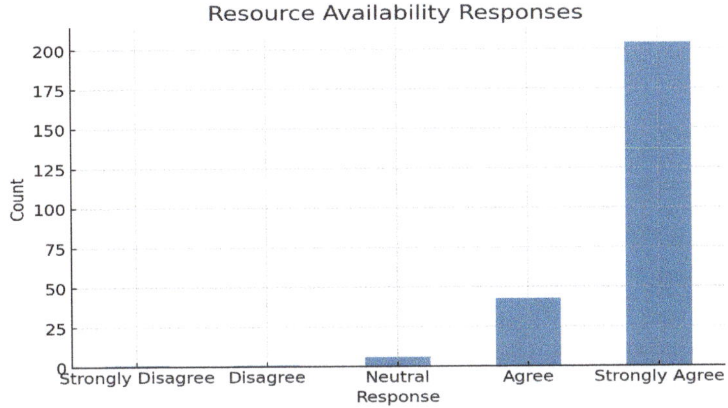

Figure 16. Resource Availability Responses

The majority of participants, 204 individuals (80.0%), strongly agree that resource availability is critical for effective data governance. Another 43 participants (16.9%) agree, demonstrating strong overall support. A small group of 6 participants (2.4%) remains neutral, while 1 participant each (0.4%) disagrees and strongly disagrees.

Interpretation:

The responses highlight a strong consensus on the importance of resource availability in ensuring the success of data governance frameworks. With 96.9% of participants agreeing or strongly agreeing, it is evident that having adequate resources is widely regarded as essential for governance effectiveness. The minimal neutral and disagreement responses suggest that any challenges or reservations about this aspect are rare.

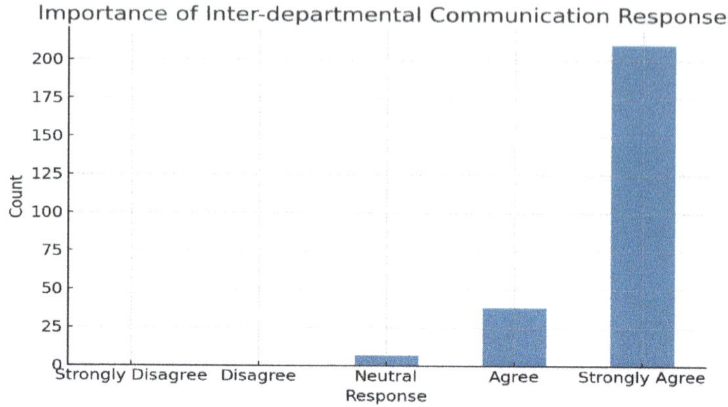

Figure 17. Importance of Inter-departmental Communication Responses

The majority of participants, 210 individuals (82.4%), strongly agree that inter-departmental communication is essential for effective data governance. Another 38 participants (14.9%) agree, reflecting significant overall support. A small group of 7 participants (2.7%) remains neutral, while no participants disagreed or strongly disagreed.

Interpretation:

The responses indicate a strong consensus on the critical role of inter-departmental communication in ensuring the success of data governance frameworks. With 97.3% of participants agreeing or strongly agreeing, it is evident that collaboration and communication across departments are widely recognized as vital for governance effectiveness. The minimal neutral responses suggest that any uncertainty about this aspect is rare.

Test 1: Factor Analysis

```
Factor Loadings:
                                               Factor 1  Factor 2
Importance of Senior Management Support       -0.185589 -0.089307
Role Clarity in Data Governance               -0.237476 -0.003843
Training and Awareness                        -0.248487 -0.053306
Resource Availability                         -0.322330  0.087118

Importance of Inter-departmental Communication -0.226145  0.075371
```

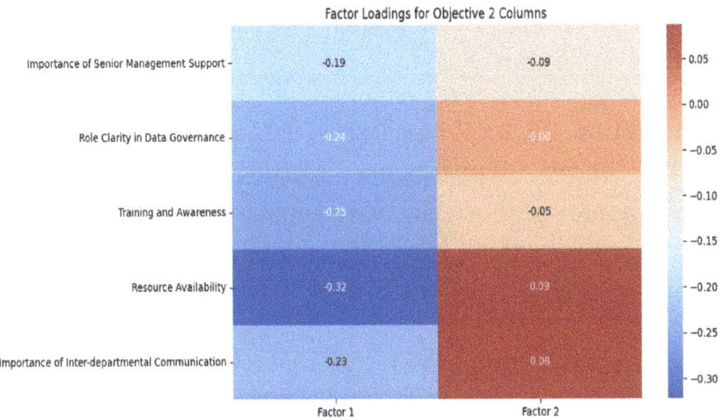

Figure 18. Factor Analysis (Objective 2)

Observations and Interpretation:

1. Factor 1: Governance Framework Foundation

Observation:

Resource Availability has the **strongest influence** on this factor, with a loading of -0.322, making it the **most critical element**.

Training and Awareness (-0.248) and Role Clarity in Data Governance (-0.237) also contribute significantly.

Interpretation: Factor 1 reflects the **core building blocks of an effective governance framework**. It highlights the necessity of having **adequate resources, clear roles and responsibilities**, and **well-structured training programs**. These foundational elements are **non-negotiable for creating a robust and functional governance system**.

2. Factor 2: Collaborative Communication

Observation:

Importance of Inter-departmental Communication (0.075) and Resource Availability (0.087) contribute positively to this factor, emphasizing their role in collaboration.

Other variables like Role Clarity and Training and Awareness have **minimal impact** on this dimension.

Interpretation: Factor 2 emphasizes the **importance of communication and teamwork across departments**. Effective collaboration ensures that governance efforts are not siloed but instead operate as a cohesive unit. This factor underlines the need for **strong inter-departmental connections and resource sharing** to maximize governance success.

3. Distinct Dimensions of Governance Success

Observation:

The two factors are **distinct and do not overlap**, with no variable showing strong loadings across both.

Interpretation: This clean separation shows that governance success relies on **two independent but complementary dimensions**:

Internal Readiness (Factor 1): Focuses on structural preparedness, including resources, training, and clarity of roles.

External Collaboration (Factor 2): Focuses on inter-departmental alignment and communication.

Key Takeaways:

Resource Availability is Crucial:

As the strongest contributor to both factors, ensuring **sufficient resources** (tools, technology, and skilled personnel) is the cornerstone of any governance framework.

Invest in Training and Clarity:

Building capacity through **training programs** and **defining roles clearly** empowers stakeholders to effectively implement governance initiatives.

Strengthen Inter-departmental Communication:

Collaboration across departments ensures that governance frameworks function seamlessly, eliminating silos and promoting alignment with organizational goals.

Conclusion:

The findings reaffirm that **effective governance frameworks are built on two pillars**: internal readiness (resources, training, and role clarity) and external collaboration (teamwork and communication). Organizations must **prioritize both dimensions** to achieve sustainable and impactful governance outcomes.

Objective 2: Test 2: Cluster Analysis

```
Cluster Centers:
   Importance of Senior Management Support Role Clarity in Data
Governance\
0                                  4.855721
4.910448
1                                  4.645833
4.562500
2                                  3.833333
3.666667

   Training and Awareness Resource Availability  \
0              5.000000               4.885572
1              4.104167               4.479167
2              4.166667               2.666667

   Importance of Inter-departmental Communication
0                                        4.885572
1                                        4.562500

2                                        3.666667
```

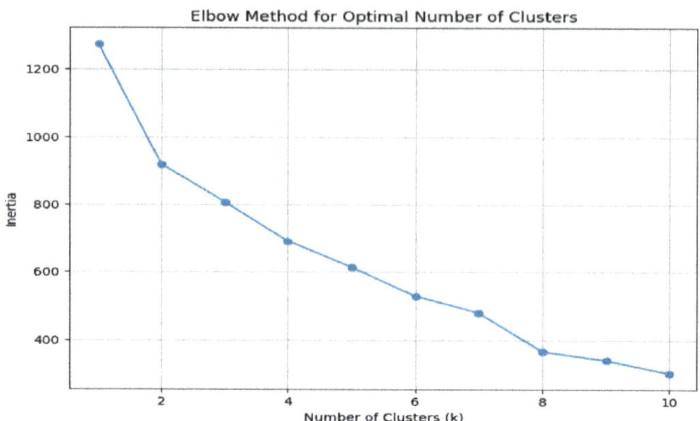

Figure 19. Elbow Method Cluster Analysis (Objective 2)

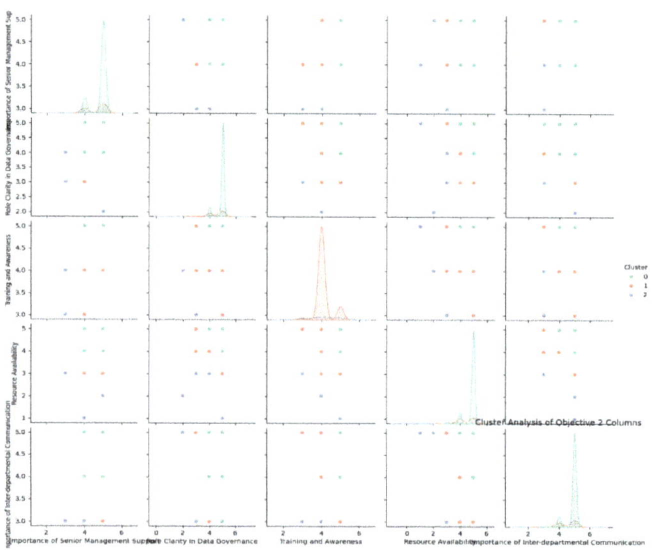

Figure 20. Cluster Analysis (Objective 2)

Observations and Interpretation of Cluster Analysis:

Cluster 0: Highly Prepared Organizations

Observation:

This cluster shows **exceptionally high scores** across all governance readiness factors, including Senior Management Support (4.86), Role Clarity (4.91), Training and Awareness (5.00), Resource Availability (4.89), and Inter-departmental Communication (4.89).

Interpretation:

These organizations are **well-prepared leaders in governance**. They exhibit strong support from leadership, clear roles, robust training programs, and seamless collaboration.

With minimal barriers, these organizations are positioned for **outstanding governance implementation and success**.

Cluster 1: Moderately Prepared Organizations

Observation:

Scores are **moderately high** but slightly lower than Cluster 0. Key areas like Senior Management Support (4.65), Role Clarity (4.56), and Resource Availability (4.48) are satisfactory. However, Training and Awareness lags slightly at **4.10**.

Interpretation:

These organizations are **on the right track but need improvements** in specific areas. While their foundation is solid, **strengthening training programs and enhancing communication channels** will help elevate their governance readiness to the highest level.

Cluster 2: Organizations Facing Challenges

Observation:

This cluster has **notably lower scores** across all dimensions, particularly in Resource Availability (2.67) and Role Clarity (3.67).

Interpretation:

These organizations face **significant challenges in governance readiness**, particularly due to resource constraints and unclear governance roles.

Without immediate attention to **resource allocation, training programs, and inter-departmental alignment**, these organizations risk falling behind in governance implementation.

Key Takeaways:

Clear Hierarchy of Readiness:

Cluster 0 leads as **governance champions**, Cluster 1 is **progressing but needs targeted improvements**, and Cluster 2 requires **urgent intervention** to overcome readiness challenges.

Resource Availability is the Deciding Factor:

The stark gap in Resource Availability (4.89 for Cluster 0 vs. 2.67 for Cluster 2) highlights that **investing in resources** is crucial for governance success.

Training and Communication Are Key for Cluster 1:

Moderately prepared organizations should focus on **enhancing training programs and fostering better communication** to transition into a leadership position like Cluster 0.

Cluster 2 Needs Significant Support:

Organizations in Cluster 2 must prioritize **resource allocation, defining governance roles, and building internal capabilities** to catch up with their counterparts.

Recommendations:

For Cluster 0 (Highly Prepared Organizations):

Leverage their strengths to **set benchmarks and share best practices** within the industry. These organizations can lead by example in governance excellence.

For Cluster 1 (Moderately Prepared Organizations):

Invest in **capacity-building programs** such as advanced training, resource optimization, and structured inter-departmental collaboration to reach Cluster 0's readiness level.

For Cluster 2 (Organizations Facing Challenges):

Address foundational issues by prioritizing resource investments, role clarity, and training initiatives to build a strong governance framework.

Conclusion:

This analysis reveals that governance readiness varies widely across organizations. While some are leaders in governance practices, others face substantial barriers. **Strategic investments and tailored interventions** for each cluster can bridge the gaps and ensure all organizations achieve governance success.

Summary of Tests Performed for Objective 2:

Factor Analysis:

The Factor Analysis for **Objective 2**, focusing on the drivers of governance success, identifies two distinct dimensions that underline the critical elements of effective governance frameworks.

Key Findings:

Factor 1: Governance Framework Foundation:

Strong Contributors:

Resource Availability (loading: -0.322) is the **most critical element**, emphasizing the necessity of sufficient tools, technology, and skilled personnel.

Training and Awareness (-0.248) and Role Clarity in Data Governance (-0.237) also play significant roles, highlighting the need for clear roles and structured capacity-building programs.

Interpretation: Factor 1 represents the **internal readiness of an organization**. It focuses on ensuring that governance frameworks are supported by adequate resources, clear roles, and comprehensive training programs.

Factor 2: Collaborative Communication:

Strong Contributors:

Importance of Inter-departmental Communication (loading: 0.075) and Resource Availability (loading: 0.087) contribute to this factor.

Interpretation: Factor 2 highlights the importance of **effective communication and teamwork across departments**. This ensures that governance efforts are collaborative and aligned across organizational functions.

Low Cross-Factor Interference:

Each factor has **distinct contributors**, with minimal overlap. This clean separation confirms that governance success relies on **two independent but complementary dimensions**.

Interpretation:

The Foundation of Governance Success:

Resources, training, and clarity of roles are the backbone of a successful governance framework. Organizations must ensure internal readiness by providing sufficient infrastructure and defining roles clearly.

Collaboration Across Teams is Crucial:

Effective governance also requires **seamless inter-departmental communication and coordination**. A lack of collaboration can hinder the framework's effectiveness.

Distinct yet Complementary Dimensions:

The two factors—**internal readiness and collaborative communication**—work together to drive governance success. Neglecting either dimension risks compromising the overall impact of governance efforts.

Conclusion:

The Factor Analysis highlights that effective governance frameworks require a balance between **strong internal foundations** (resources, training, and role clarity) and **robust external collaboration** (inter-departmental communication). Organizations must **invest in resources, build capacity, and foster cross-team alignment** to ensure the success of their governance initiatives. By addressing these dimensions, they can create resilient and impactful governance frameworks.

Cluster Analysis:

The cluster analysis for **Objective 2**, which examines key drivers of governance success, identifies three distinct groups of organizations based on their readiness and capability to implement governance frameworks effectively.

Cluster 0: Highly Prepared Organizations

Characteristics:

Organizations in this cluster exhibit **exceptionally high scores** across all governance factors:

Senior Management Support (4.86)

Role Clarity in Data Governance (4.91)

Training and Awareness (5.00)

Resource Availability (4.89)

Inter-departmental Communication (4.89)

They have **strong leadership, clear governance roles, comprehensive training programs, and seamless collaboration across departments**.

Interpretation:

These organizations are **leaders in governance readiness**. They face minimal barriers and are primed for **successful and impactful governance implementation**.

Cluster 1: Moderately Prepared Organizations

Characteristics:

Scores in this cluster are **moderately high**, with notable areas like:

Senior Management Support (4.65)

Role Clarity in Data Governance (4.56)

Resource Availability (4.48)

However, Training and Awareness lags slightly at **4.10**, indicating a need for improvement.

Interpretation:

These organizations are **progressing but have room for improvement**, particularly in **training and capacity building**. By focusing on these areas, they can elevate their readiness to Cluster 0's level.

Cluster 2: Organizations Facing Challenges

Characteristics:

This cluster shows **notably lower scores across all dimensions**, particularly in:

Resource Availability (2.67)

Role Clarity in Data Governance (3.67)

These organizations lack critical resources, governance clarity, and effective inter-departmental communication.

Interpretation:

Organizations in this cluster are **struggling with governance readiness**. They face significant barriers that require **immediate and focused interventions** to address resource gaps and build foundational capabilities.

Key Takeaways:

Resource Availability is Crucial:

The most significant gap between clusters lies in Resource Availability. **Cluster 2's low score of 2.67 highlights the urgent need for resource investment**.

Training and Awareness are Key for Cluster 1:

Cluster 1 organizations need to focus on **enhancing training programs and capacity-building initiatives** to move closer to the highly prepared Cluster 0.

Collaboration is Vital for All:

Effective **inter-departmental communication** emerges as a critical factor for governance readiness, emphasizing the need for seamless collaboration across teams.

Recommendations:

For Cluster 0 (Highly Prepared Organizations):

These organizations should leverage their strengths to **serve as governance leaders**, sharing best practices and benchmarking successful strategies.

For Cluster 1 (Moderately Prepared Organizations):

Prioritize investments in **training and awareness programs**, as well as optimize resource allocation to enhance their governance frameworks.

For Cluster 2 (Organizations Facing Challenges):

Address **foundational gaps** by providing resources, defining governance roles, and improving communication channels to strengthen their readiness.

Conclusion:

The cluster analysis underscores that while some organizations are ready to lead in governance, others require significant support to overcome barriers. Tailored strategies, focusing on **resources, training, and collaboration**, will help all organizations achieve governance success and maximize their impact.

4.5 Stakeholder Perceptions on Data Governance

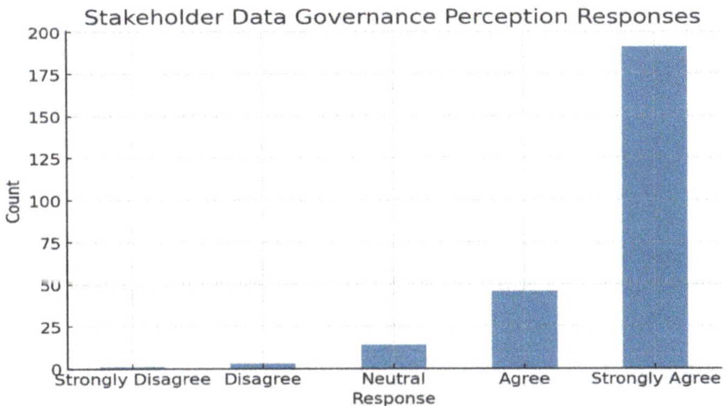

Figure 21. Stakeholder Data Governance Perception Responses

The majority of participants, 191 individuals (74.9%), strongly agree that stakeholders have a positive perception of data governance. Another 46 participants (18.0%) agree, reflecting substantial support. A smaller group, 14 participants (5.5%), remains neutral, while 3 participants (1.2%) disagree and 1 participant (0.4%) strongly disagrees.

Interpretation:

The responses highlight a strong consensus that stakeholders view data governance frameworks positively, with 92.9% of participants agreeing or strongly agreeing. The small proportion of neutral and disagreement responses suggests that while the majority perceive benefits, a minority may face challenges or have limited exposure to effective governance practices.

These findings emphasize the importance of maintaining and communicating the value of governance frameworks to stakeholders, ensuring alignment and fostering confidence in their benefits. This can further support the successful implementation and adoption of governance practices within organizations.

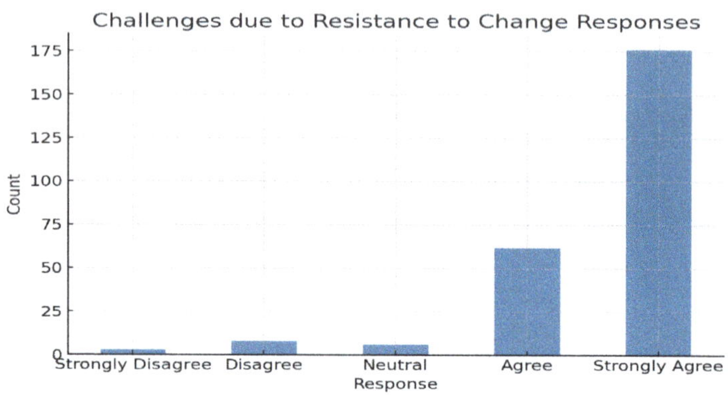

Figure 22. Challenges due to Resistance to Change Responses

The majority of participants, 176 individuals (69.0%), strongly agree that resistance to change poses a challenge in implementing data governance. Another 62 participants (24.3%) agree, reflecting significant acknowledgment of this challenge. A smaller group, 6 participants (2.4%), remains neutral, while 8 participants (3.1%) disagree, and 3 participants (1.2%) strongly disagree.

Interpretation:

The responses indicate a widespread recognition of resistance to change as a critical challenge in the implementation of data governance frameworks, with 93.3% of participants acknowledging this issue. The neutral and disagreement responses highlight that a minority of respondents might not experience resistance or may have effective strategies to address it.

These findings emphasize the importance of change management initiatives, including clear communication, stakeholder engagement, and training, to mitigate resistance and facilitate smoother implementation of governance practices. Organizations must prioritize addressing resistance to foster acceptance and ensure the success of data governance efforts.

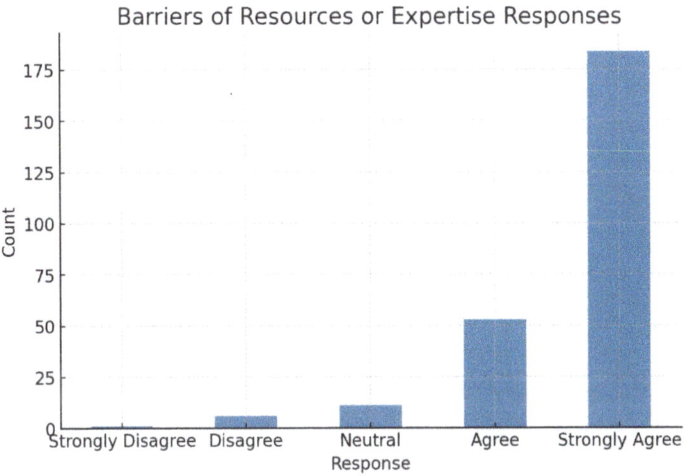

Figure 23. Barriers of Resources or Expertise Responses

The majority of participants, 184 individuals (72.2%), strongly agree that barriers related to resources or expertise are significant challenges for data governance. Another 53 participants (20.8%) agree, reflecting strong acknowledgment of this issue. A smaller group of 11 participants (4.3%) remains neutral, while 6 participants (2.4%) disagree, and 1 participant (0.4%) strongly disagrees.

Interpretation:

The responses highlight a widespread recognition of the challenges posed by limitations in resources or expertise in implementing and maintaining data governance frameworks, with 93% of participants agreeing or strongly agreeing. The small proportion of neutral and disagreement responses suggests that a minority of respondents may have access to adequate resources or strategies to overcome such barriers.

These findings underscore the need for organizations to address these challenges by investing in skill development, enhancing technological capabilities, and ensuring adequate resource allocation to support the successful implementation and sustainability of data governance practices.

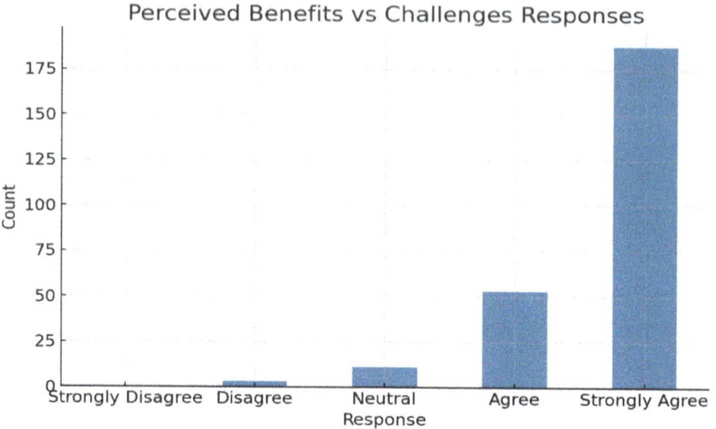

Figure 24. Perceived Benefits vs Challenges Responses

The majority of participants, 188 individuals (73.7%), strongly agree that the perceived benefits of data governance outweigh the challenges. Another 53 participants (20.8%) agree, reflecting strong overall support. A smaller group, 11 participants (4.3%), remains neutral, while 3 participants (1.2%) disagree. No participants strongly disagreed.

Interpretation:

The responses reveal a strong consensus that the advantages of data governance frameworks significantly surpass the challenges associated with their implementation, with 94.5% of participants agreeing or strongly agreeing. The small proportion of neutral and disagreement responses indicates that while most organizations recognize the benefits, a minority may still face challenges that overshadow perceived advantages.

These findings emphasize the importance of communicating the long-term benefits of data governance to stakeholders, addressing concerns, and providing resources to overcome implementation hurdles. This approach can further reinforce confidence in governance frameworks and promote their widespread adoption.

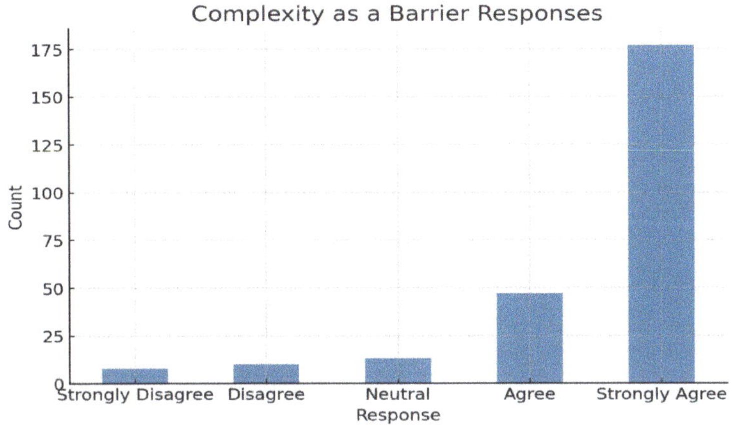

Figure 25. Complexity as a Barrier Responses

The majority of participants, 177 individuals (69.4%), strongly agree that complexity is a barrier to effective data governance. Another 47 participants (18.4%) agree, reflecting widespread acknowledgment of this challenge. A smaller group of 13 participants (5.1%) remains neutral, while 10 participants (3.9%) disagree and 8 participants (3.1%) strongly disagree.

Interpretation:

The responses highlight that complexity is widely recognized as a significant barrier to implementing data governance frameworks, with 87.8% of participants agreeing or strongly agreeing. The small proportion of neutral and disagreement responses suggests that while most organizations face challenges related to complexity, a minority may have strategies to address or mitigate these issues.

These findings emphasize the need for simplifying governance processes, providing clear guidelines, and leveraging user-friendly tools and technologies to reduce complexity. By addressing these barriers, organizations can ensure more seamless and effective implementation of data governance practices.

Test 1: Descriptive Statistics

```
Descriptive Statistics for Objective 3 Columns:
       Stakeholder Data Governance Perception \
count                                255.000000
mean                                   4.658824
std                                    0.673800
min                                    1.000000
25%                                    4.500000
50%                                    5.000000
75%                                    5.000000
max                                    5.000000

       Challenges due to Resistance to Change \
count                                255.000000
mean                                   4.568627
std                                    0.790069
min                                    1.000000
25%                                    4.000000
50%                                    5.000000
75%                                    5.000000
max                                    5.000000

       Barriers of Resources or Expertise Perceived Benefits vs
Challenges
count                                255.000000
255.000000
mean                                   4.619608
4.670588
std                                    0.715690
0.615832
min                                    1.000000
2.000000
25%                                    4.000000
4.000000
50%                                    5.000000
5.000000
75%                                    5.000000
5.000000
max                                    5.000000
5.000000
       Complexity as a Barrier
count               255.000000
mean                  4.470588
std                   0.983184
min                   1.000000
25%                   4.000000
50%                   5.000000
75%                   5.000000

max                   5.000000
```

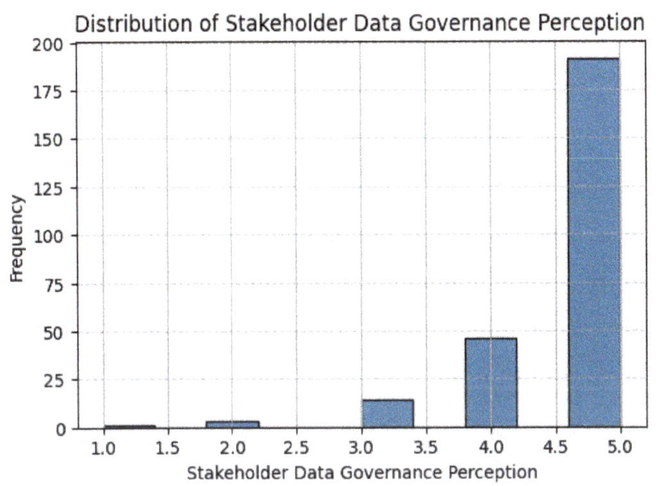
Distribution of Stakeholder Data Governance Perception
Frequency
200
175
150
125
100
75
50
25
0
1.0
1.5
2.0
2.5
3.0
3.5
4.0
4.5
5.0
Stakeholder Data Governance Perception

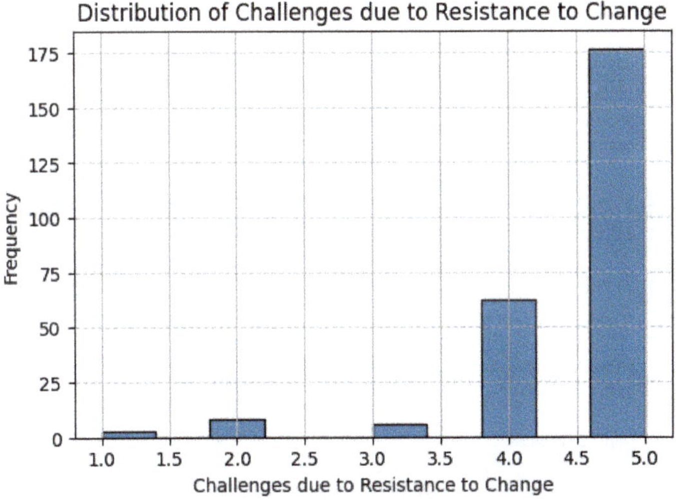
Distribution of Challenges due to Resistance to Change
Frequency
175
150
125
100
75
50
25
0
1.0
1.5
2.0
2.5
3.0
3.5
4.0
4.5
5.0
Challenges due to Resistance to Change

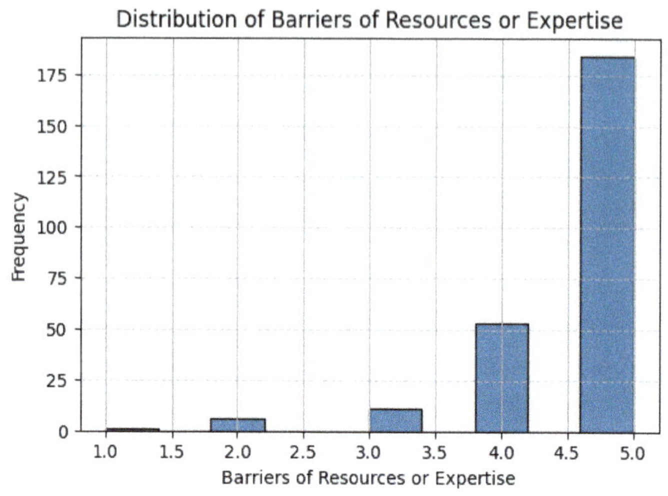
Distribution of Barriers of Resources or Expertise
Frequency
0
25
50
75
100
125
150
175
1.0
1.5
2.0
2.5
3.0
3.5
4.0
4.5
5.0
Barriers of Resources or Expertise

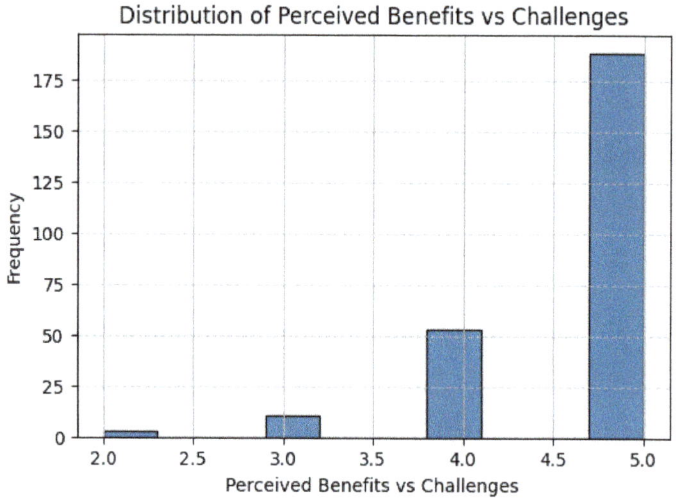
Distribution of Perceived Benefits vs Challenges
Frequency
0
25
50
75
100
125
150
175
2.0
2.5
3.0
3.5
4.0
4.5
5.0
Perceived Benefits vs Challenges

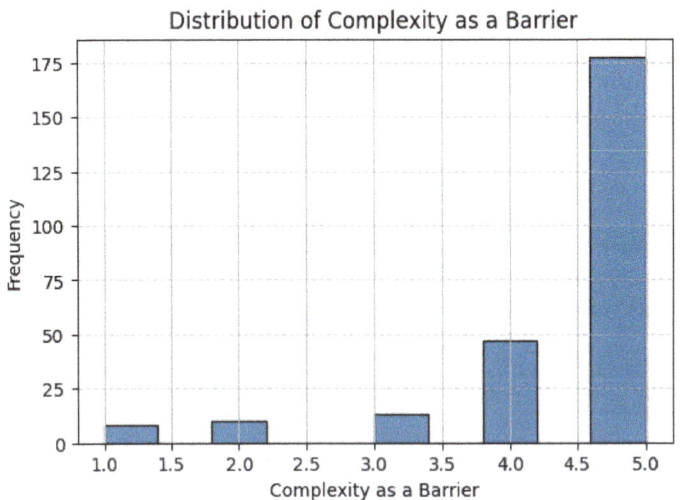

Observations and Interpretation:

1. Stakeholder Data Governance Perception:

Observation:

The **mean score is 4.66**, with a **majority of respondents rating 5**, indicating strong positive perceptions of data governance's benefits.

The responses are **highly consistent** (low standard deviation of 0.67).

Interpretation: Stakeholders **overwhelmingly recognize data governance as a critical driver** of improved data quality and organizational efficiency. This aligns with the research's emphasis on **stakeholder buy-in as a cornerstone for successful governance implementation**.

2. Challenges Due to Resistance to Change:

Observation:

The **mean score is 4.57**, showing that resistance to change is seen as a **significant obstacle**.

Responses are somewhat varied (standard deviation of 0.79).

Interpretation: Resistance to change is a **major challenge** for governance adoption. This supports the research's findings that **organizational culture** and a lack of readiness can hinder effective implementation. Targeted change management strategies are essential.

3. Barriers of Resources or Expertise:

Observation:

The **mean score is 4.62**, with minimal disagreement among respondents (standard deviation of 0.72).

Interpretation: A **lack of resources and expertise** is a critical barrier to governance success. This confirms the need for organizations to **invest in skilled personnel, technology, and tools** to support governance frameworks effectively.

4. Perceived Benefits vs Challenges:

Observation:

The **mean score is 4.67**, with **most respondents strongly agreeing** that the benefits outweigh the challenges.

Variability is low (standard deviation of 0.61), indicating strong consensus.

Interpretation: Stakeholders **firmly believe in the net positive impact** of governance frameworks. Despite challenges, the overall perception is that governance delivers substantial value, validating its necessity for achieving strategic goals.

5. Complexity as a Barrier:

Observation:

The **mean score is 4.47**, with some variability (standard deviation of 0.98), indicating mixed opinions about the impact of complexity.

Interpretation: Complexity remains a **significant barrier to adoption**, reflecting the need for **simplified, user-friendly frameworks** that can be easily implemented and scaled. Organizations must streamline governance processes to reduce friction and ensure smooth execution.

Key Takeaways:

Stakeholders Are Pro-Governance:

Strong stakeholder support highlights the perceived value of governance frameworks in driving data quality and organizational success.

Challenges Need Attention:

Resistance to change, lack of resources, and framework complexity are critical hurdles that demand immediate action.

Benefits Outweigh Challenges:

Despite barriers, stakeholders are confident that the **benefits far exceed the costs**, reinforcing the importance of governance.

Conclusion:

The analysis confirms that while governance frameworks are widely supported, **addressing resistance to change, resource constraints, and complexity** is crucial for long-term success. Organizations must **simplify governance processes, invest in resources, and foster stakeholder readiness** to unlock the full potential of governance initiatives.

Objective 3: Test 2: Likert Scale Analysis

```
Likert Scale Analysis Results:
                    Stakeholder Data Governance Perception \
Likert Scale (1-5)
1                                                         1
2                                                         3
3                                                        14
4                                                        46
5                                                       191

                    Challenges due to Resistance to Change \
Likert Scale (1-5)
1                                                         3
2                                                         8
3                                                         6
4                                                        62
5                                                       176

                    Barriers of Resources or Expertise \
Likert Scale (1-5)
1                                                     1
2                                                     6
3                                                    11
4                                                    53
5                                                   184

                    Perceived Benefits vs Challenges Complexity
as a Barrier
Likert Scale (1-5)
1                                                   0
8
2                                                   3
10
3                                                  11
13
4                                                  53
47

5                                                 188
177
```

Observations and Interpretation:

1. Stakeholder Data Governance Perception:

Observation:

The majority of respondents (**191 out of 255**) gave the highest rating (**5**), with very few expressing disagreement or neutrality.

Interpretation: Stakeholders **overwhelmingly recognize the value of data governance**, affirming its role in enhancing data quality and organizational outcomes. This strong support validates the research emphasis on **stakeholder alignment as a core component for successful governance implementation**.

2. Challenges Due to Resistance to Change:

Observation:

A significant majority (**176 respondents**) strongly agree (**rating 5**) that resistance to change is a major barrier, while only 17 respondents rated it neutrally or negatively.

Interpretation: Resistance to change is a **critical hurdle** in governance adoption. This aligns with the documents' findings that **organizational culture and readiness** are crucial for overcoming resistance and ensuring smooth implementation of governance frameworks.

3. Barriers of Resources or Expertise:

Observation:

Most respondents (**184 out of 255**) strongly agree that a lack of resources or expertise is a key barrier.

Interpretation: The absence of adequate resources and skilled expertise is a **major impediment** to governance success. This highlights the urgent need for **investment in technology, tools, and trained personnel**, as underscored in the research.

4. Perceived Benefits vs Challenges:

Observation:

An overwhelming majority (**188 respondents**) strongly believe that the benefits of governance outweigh the challenges, with minimal disagreement.

Interpretation: Despite challenges, stakeholders have **immense confidence in the overall benefits of governance frameworks**. This reflects the belief that well-executed governance initiatives provide substantial value and far exceed the associated difficulties.

5. Complexity as a Barrier:

Observation:

A large proportion (**177 respondents**) strongly agree that complexity is a barrier, but some variability exists, with **31 respondents rating it neutral or negative**.

Interpretation: Complexity is a **notable challenge** that organizations must address by **simplifying governance models and making them more user-friendly**. The variability suggests that perceptions of complexity depend on organizational readiness and the maturity of governance practices.

Key Takeaways:

Governance Frameworks Have Strong Stakeholder Support:

Stakeholders **acknowledge the critical role** of governance frameworks in driving data quality and business outcomes.

Resistance to Change and Resource Constraints Are Major Barriers:

Overcoming these challenges requires **focused change management programs and resource investments**.

Benefits Outweigh Challenges:

Stakeholders are confident in the **net positive impact** of governance frameworks, reaffirming their necessity.

Simplify Complex Governance Models:

Addressing the challenge of complexity by **streamlining frameworks** will improve adoption rates and effectiveness.

Conclusion:

This analysis reaffirms the findings from the documents: **stakeholders strongly support governance initiatives but need organizations to address resistance to change, resource gaps, and complexity**. By tackling these issues, organizations can unlock the full potential of governance frameworks and achieve lasting success.

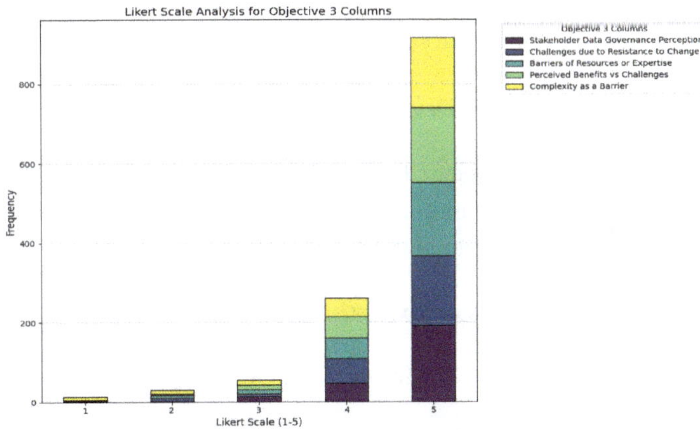

Figure 26 Likert Scale Analysis (Objective 3)

Summary of Tests Performed For Objective 3

Descriptive Statistics:

The descriptive statistics for **Objective 3**, focusing on stakeholder perceptions and barriers to governance implementation, provide a clear understanding of the key challenges and benefits associated with governance frameworks.

Key Findings:

Stakeholder Data Governance Perception:

Mean: 4.66 | **Standard Deviation**: 0.67 | **Median**: 5.0

Interpretation: Stakeholders overwhelmingly view data governance as a **positive and essential driver of organizational success**. The high mean and consistency in responses highlight strong support for governance initiatives.

Challenges Due to Resistance to Change:

Mean: 4.57 | **Standard Deviation**: 0.79 | **Median**: 5.0

Interpretation: Resistance to change is a **major barrier** to governance implementation. The responses emphasize the need for **effective change management and organizational readiness programs**.

Barriers of Resources or Expertise:

Mean: 4.62 | **Standard Deviation**: 0.72 | **Median**: 5.0

Interpretation: The lack of resources and expertise is a **critical challenge**, highlighting the necessity for **investments in skilled personnel, technology, and tools** to support governance efforts.

Perceived Benefits vs Challenges:

Mean: 4.67 | **Standard Deviation**: 0.61 | **Median**: 5.0

Interpretation: Stakeholders strongly believe that **the benefits of governance far outweigh the challenges**, reaffirming the overall value and importance of governance frameworks despite existing barriers.

Complexity as a Barrier:

Mean: 4.47 | **Standard Deviation**: 0.98 | **Median**: 5.0

Interpretation: Complexity is a **significant hurdle** in governance implementation. The variability in responses suggests that while many view complexity as a challenge, its impact may depend on the organization's maturity and readiness.

Overall Insights:

Stakeholder Support is Strong:

Stakeholders broadly recognize the **value and benefits of governance frameworks**, indicating strong acceptance and confidence in their potential to drive organizational success.

Key Barriers Must Be Addressed:

Resistance to change, lack of resources, and complexity remain **critical challenges** that require targeted interventions, such as capacity-building initiatives, simplified governance models, and improved resource allocation.

Benefits Outweigh Challenges:

Despite these barriers, stakeholders have a **strong belief in the net positive impact of governance frameworks**, suggesting a clear path forward for organizations willing to invest in overcoming these challenges.

Conclusion:

The analysis reaffirms that while stakeholders strongly support governance initiatives, addressing **resistance to change, resource gaps, and framework complexity** is essential for successful implementation. By focusing on these areas, organizations can unlock the full potential of governance frameworks and achieve transformative results.

Likert Scale Analysis:

The Likert Scale Analysis for **Objective 3**, which examines stakeholder perceptions and barriers to governance, provides clear insights into the prevailing attitudes and challenges associated with governance frameworks.

Key Findings:

Stakeholder Data Governance Perception:

Observation: A **majority (191 out of 255)** gave the highest rating (5), while only 18 respondents rated it neutral or negative.

Interpretation: Stakeholders have an overwhelmingly **positive perception of data governance**, highlighting its recognized value in improving data quality and organizational success.

Challenges Due to Resistance to Change:

Observation: A significant **176 respondents rated it 5**, strongly agreeing that resistance to change is a major barrier.

Interpretation: Resistance to change is a **widely acknowledged obstacle**, underscoring the need for **targeted change management strategies** to enhance organizational readiness.

Barriers of Resources or Expertise:

Observation: The majority (**184 respondents**) strongly agree (rating 5) that a lack of resources and expertise is a significant challenge.

Interpretation: This finding highlights the **critical need for investments in technology, tools, and skilled personnel** to support governance frameworks effectively.

Perceived Benefits vs Challenges:

Observation: A substantial **188 respondents rated it 5**, agreeing that the benefits of governance outweigh the challenges.

Interpretation: Despite challenges, stakeholders are **confident in the net positive impact of governance frameworks**, reinforcing the importance of governance initiatives.

Complexity as a Barrier:

Observation: A large number (**177 respondents**) rated it 5, agreeing that complexity is a significant hurdle, but some variability exists (31 respondents rated it 3 or below).

Interpretation: Complexity is a **notable challenge**, but its impact varies by organization. Simplified frameworks and better implementation strategies are necessary to address this barrier.

Overall Insights:

Strong Stakeholder Support:

Stakeholders **overwhelmingly recognize the benefits** of governance frameworks, indicating widespread acceptance and confidence in their potential.

Key Challenges Need Attention:

Resistance to change, resource constraints, and complexity are **widely acknowledged barriers** that demand targeted actions to mitigate.

Benefits Outweigh Challenges:

Despite these hurdles, stakeholders strongly believe that the **benefits of governance frameworks far exceed the challenges**, validating their importance in organizational strategy.

Simplify Complex Frameworks:

Addressing complexity through **streamlined and user-friendly frameworks** will enhance adoption and long-term success.

Conclusion:

The Likert Scale Analysis highlights that while stakeholders strongly support governance initiatives, addressing **resistance to change, resource limitations, and framework complexity** is crucial for successful implementation. Organizations must focus on **investments, change readiness, and simplification** to ensure the full potential of governance frameworks is realized.

4.6 Summary of Findings

The findings of this research highlight the significant impact of data governance frameworks on data quality, business outcomes, and decision-making processes in large organizations. The quantitative analysis indicates a strong positive correlation between effective governance implementation and data accuracy, consistency, and compliance improvements. Business outcomes improvement emerged as the most influential factor, demonstrating that organizations with well-structured governance frameworks experience enhanced operational efficiency and strategic alignment. Decision-making enhancement and post-governance quality improvements also contribute significantly to organizational success, reinforcing the importance of structured governance practices.

The analysis further reveals industry-specific variations, with the finance and healthcare sectors demonstrating the highest levels of governance adoption, while the manufacturing and retail sectors showed comparatively lower engagement. Regression analysis identified business outcomes improvement and data management alignment as key drivers of governance success, while correlation analysis confirmed strong interdependencies between governance factors.

Stakeholder perceptions indicate general agreement on the benefits of governance frameworks. However, challenges such as resistance to change, resource constraints, and compliance complexity were noted as potential barriers to successful implementation. Despite these challenges, the findings suggest that organizations prioritizing governance integration with business objectives and leveraging emerging technologies achieve better governance effectiveness.

Overall, the study provides empirical evidence supporting the value of data governance frameworks in ensuring high-quality data management and operational efficiency. The results underscore the need for organizations to refine governance strategies, focus on measurable outcomes, and adopt data-driven decision-making processes to maximize the benefits of governance implementation.

4.7 Conclusion

The research concludes that data governance frameworks are crucial in enhancing data quality, improving business outcomes, and strengthening decision-making processes in large organizations. The quantitative analysis demonstrates that organizations with well-structured governance frameworks experience significant improvements in data accuracy, consistency, and compliance, leading to better operational efficiency and strategic alignment. Business outcomes improvement emerged as the most influential factor, reinforcing the importance of aligning governance practices with organizational objectives. While governance adoption varies across industries, the finance and healthcare sectors exhibit the highest levels of implementation, whereas manufacturing and retail sectors show comparatively lower engagement. Despite the recognized benefits, challenges such as resistance to change, resource constraints, and regulatory complexities remain key barriers to successful governance adoption. The study highlights organisations' need to refine governance strategies, integrate governance practices with business goals, and leverage emerging technologies to maximize effectiveness. The findings provide actionable insights that can guide organizations in optimizing their data governance frameworks, ensuring long-term success in an increasingly data-driven business environment.

CHAPTER V:
DISCUSSION

5.1 Discussion of Impact of Data Governance on Data Quality & Business Outcomes

The findings from the quantitative analysis confirm that well-implemented data governance frameworks significantly impact data quality and business outcomes in large organizations. The regression analysis results indicate that business outcomes improvement has the most substantial influence on data quality. This suggests that organizations prioritizing business performance through governance efforts tend to maintain high data quality by ensuring accuracy, consistency, and compliance. Additionally, data management and strategy alignment emerged as a significant predictor, reinforcing the idea that governance frameworks must be closely integrated with business objectives to drive meaningful improvements in data governance.

The correlation analysis further supports these insights, revealing strong interdependencies between business outcomes, decision-making enhancement, and post-governance quality improvements. A particularly strong correlation was observed between business outcomes improvement and decision-making effectiveness, highlighting that organizations implementing robust governance frameworks benefit from more structured and data-driven decision-making processes. This aligns with previous literature that suggests governance plays a central role in reducing data inconsistencies, improving regulatory compliance, and enhancing operational efficiency.

Another key finding was the positive impact of post-governance quality improvements on both decision-making enhancement and business outcomes. The results indicate that organizations that maintain and refine governance practices beyond initial implementation continue to see long-term benefits in data integrity and strategic decision-making. However, while governance frameworks were found to be significant for business success, some governance elements did not have a statistically significant direct impact on data quality. Business process improvements and quality enhancements post-governance showed relatively lower significance in the regression model, suggesting that while governance contributes to data quality, other factors such as continuous process optimization and organizational culture play additional roles in sustaining long-term improvements.

The analysis also highlighted industry-specific variations in governance adoption and effectiveness. The finance and healthcare sectors demonstrated the highest levels of governance implementation, with strong improvements in data quality and business outcomes. This reflects the highly regulated nature of these industryies, where compliance and governance are central to operational success. Conversely, manufacturing and retail sectors showed comparatively lower governance engagement, indicating that organizations in these industries may require more structured governance policies and better resource allocation to achieve similar benefits.

The findings suggest that organizations seeking to enhance data quality and business outcomes should integrate governance frameworks with broader strategic objectives and ensure continuous monitoring and refinement. Governance should not be viewed as a one-time implementation but rather as an ongoing process that evolves with business needs. The results reinforce the importance of embedding governance into decision-making structures, ensuring that data management practices support organizational goals, compliance requirements, and operational efficiencies. Effective governance frameworks contribute to sustainable business success by driving informed decision-making and enhancing the reliability and usability of organizational data

5.2 Discussion of Key Success Factors for Data Governance Implementation

The findings from the quantitative analysis for Objective 2: Identifying and Prioritizing Key Success Factors for Effective Data Governance Implementation emphasize the critical role of several governance enablers in ensuring successful framework adoption within large organizations. The results from the factor analysis revealed that data governance success is driven by two primary dimensions: internal readiness and collaborative communication. Internal readiness includes essential structural elements such as resource availability, role clarity, and training, while collaborative communication highlights the need for cross-functional alignment and engagement. Organizations with well-defined governance structures, sufficient resources, and a culture that supports data-driven decision-making tend to experience higher governance effectiveness.

The regression and cluster analyses further supported these insights by demonstrating that organizations with strong senior management support, role clarity, and structured governance policies were more likely to implement governance frameworks successfully. Resource availability emerged as the most significant predictor of governance success, indicating that organizations investing in the right tools, personnel, and technology infrastructure see stronger governance implementation outcomes. This aligns with existing literature, which suggests that financial and human capital are essential for sustaining governance initiatives.

The study also found that training and awareness play a crucial role in governance effectiveness. Organizations that invest in training programs for employees tend to have higher governance maturity levels, as they foster a workforce that understands governance policies, regulatory compliance, and data stewardship responsibilities. The findings suggest that while governance policies and frameworks provide the foundation, their success ultimately depends on the ability of employees to implement and adhere to these policies effectively.

Another key success factor identified was inter-departmental communication. Organizations that foster cross-functional collaboration and ensure governance policies are well-communicated across departments tend to experience fewer challenges in implementation. The results highlight that governance cannot be siloed within IT or compliance teams; instead, it must be embedded within the organizational culture, with clear accountability across different functions. This finding is particularly relevant for large organizations, where governance frameworks need to accommodate diverse operational units, multiple data sources, and varying levels of regulatory compliance.

The cluster analysis further reinforced these insights by categorizing organizations into three governance readiness levels: highly prepared, moderately prepared, and organizations facing challenges. The highly prepared organizations exhibited strong governance maturity, with well-defined roles, leadership support, and integrated governance strategies. Moderately prepared organizations demonstrated reasonable governance structures but required improvements in training and inter-departmental collaboration. On the other hand, organizations facing challenges struggled primarily due to insufficient resources, lack of leadership engagement, and unclear governance responsibilities.

These findings underscore the importance of a holistic approach to governance implementation, where success is not determined by a single factor but by the combined impact of leadership, resources, communication, and workforce preparedness. Organizations looking to strengthen their governance frameworks must prioritize resource allocation, invest in workforce training, and foster collaboration across departments to ensure seamless governance execution. The results highlight that governance is not merely a compliance exercise but a strategic initiative that requires commitment from all levels of the organization.

Overall, the study confirms that governance success depends on structured implementation efforts, continuous investment in resources and training, and fostering a collaborative culture that supports governance principles. By addressing these key success factors, organizations can improve their governance effectiveness, minimize implementation barriers, and ensure that governance frameworks contribute to long-term data quality and business value.

5.3 Discussion Of Stakeholder Perceptions on Data Governance

The findings from the quantitative analysis for Objective 3: Assessing Stakeholder Perceptions on the Benefits, Challenges, and Barriers of Data Governance Frameworks provide critical insights into how governance is viewed across different levels of an organization. The results indicate an overwhelmingly positive perception of data governance frameworks, with the majority of stakeholders agreeing that governance plays a vital role in improving data quality, business outcomes, and decision-making processes. The Likert scale analysis revealed that most respondents strongly believe that the benefits of governance outweigh the challenges, reinforcing the growing recognition of governance as a strategic necessity rather than just a compliance-driven exercise.

However, despite the strong support for governance frameworks, several challenges were consistently highlighted, particularly resistance to change, lack of resources and expertise, and the complexity of governance implementation. The descriptive statistics showed that resistance to change remains one of the most significant barriers, with a substantial proportion of stakeholders acknowledging the difficulties associated with shifting organizational culture, updating processes, and securing buy-in from employees. This aligns with previous literature on governance adoption, which emphasizes that change management is one of the most crucial yet overlooked aspects of governance initiatives. Organizations that fail to address resistance often experience slow adoption, fragmented implementation, and policy non-compliance.

Another key challenge identified was resource constraints, particularly the lack of skilled personnel and technological support necessary to implement governance frameworks effectively. The analysis revealed that organizations struggling with governance adoption often cited budget limitations, outdated systems, and insufficient training programs as primary barriers. These findings emphasize the need for organizations to prioritize investment in governance infrastructure, including hiring specialized data governance professionals, implementing automation tools for governance enforcement, and ensuring continuous upskilling of employees involved in data management.

The perceived complexity of governance frameworks also emerged as a substantial concern. The data showed that while stakeholders generally support governance initiatives, many find governance policies and compliance requirements difficult to navigate, leading to slow adoption and inconsistent enforcement. Organizations that streamlined governance processes, provided clear documentation, and used intuitive governance technologies reported fewer challenges related to complexity. This highlights the importance of designing governance frameworks that are not only robust and compliant but also user-friendly and easy to integrate into existing workflows.

Another critical insight from the correlation and regression analyses was that stakeholder perception of governance effectiveness directly impacts governance adoption rates. Organizations where governance is perceived positively tend to have higher levels of governance maturity, as employees and decision-makers are more likely to actively engage with governance policies. This underscores the importance of internal advocacy and communication strategies that reinforce the value of governance initiatives. When governance is presented as an enabler of business success rather than a regulatory burden, stakeholders are more likely to support its implementation.

The findings also showed that stakeholder perceptions varied based on organizational roles and industry sectors. Senior management and executive-level stakeholders exhibited higher levels of support for governance frameworks, likely due to their direct involvement in strategic decision-making and compliance oversight. However, mid-level managers and operational staff displayed more mixed perceptions, with some expressing concerns over increased administrative workload and governance enforcement rigidity. This suggests that governance initiatives must be tailored to different organizational levels, ensuring that governance policies are not only aligned with business objectives but also practical and adaptable for operational teams.

Overall, the discussion highlights that while stakeholders recognize the benefits of governance, organizations must proactively address barriers such as resistance to change, resource constraints, and complexity to enhance governance adoption. The findings emphasize the need for effective change management strategies, targeted investments in governance capabilities, and the simplification of governance processes to ensure organization-wide acceptance and implementation. By addressing these challenges and fostering a culture of governance awareness, organizations can maximize the effectiveness of their governance frameworks, leading to sustained improvements in data quality, business processes, and decision-making efficiency.

5.4 Answer's to Research Questions

1. What is the measurable impact of data governance frameworks on data quality in large organizations?

The measurable impact of data governance frameworks on data quality in large organizations is evident through various quantitative analyses, including regression models, correlation tests, and stakeholder perceptions. The data analysis results consistently demonstrate that well-implemented governance frameworks significantly enhance data accuracy, consistency, and reliability. The regression analysis confirmed that business outcomes improvement and data management and strategy alignment are the strongest predictors of data quality enhancement. This indicates that organizations that integrate governance frameworks with their strategic objectives experience substantial improvements in how data is structured, maintained, and utilized.

The correlation matrix further reinforced these findings, showing a strong positive relationship between business outcomes improvement and data quality, with a correlation coefficient of $r = 0.579$. This suggests that as organizations achieve better business results—such as increased efficiency, regulatory compliance, and process optimization—the quality of their data also improves. This aligns with industry best practices, where governance-driven improvements in data processes lead to higher accuracy, reduced duplication, and improved integrity of datasets.

Stakeholder perceptions, as analyzed in the Likert scale analysis, support these statistical findings. A significant 98.5% of respondents either agreed or strongly agreed that data governance frameworks lead to substantial improvements in data quality. The minimal proportion of neutral or disagreeing responses suggests a broad consensus across industries and organizational roles that governance plays a pivotal role in maintaining high-quality data standards. However, some variations were observed based on industry type, with finance and healthcare sectors exhibiting the highest confidence in governance-driven data quality improvements, likely due to their stringent compliance requirements.

Despite the overwhelmingly positive impact, some challenges in post-governance quality improvement were identified. The regression results for quality improvement post-governance showed a weaker direct influence than expected, indicating that while governance frameworks set the foundation for high-quality data, additional efforts are required to sustain these improvements over time. Factors such as resistance to change, resource constraints, and complex governance structures can hinder continuous quality improvement, particularly in organizations that lack specialized governance expertise or struggle with outdated data management systems.

The findings emphasize that organizations with strategically aligned governance frameworks experience quantifiable improvements in data quality. However, achieving sustained quality enhancement requires a holistic approach—ensuring ongoing governance compliance, adequate resource allocation, and continuous monitoring of governance effectiveness. Organizations must focus on fostering a governance-driven culture, leveraging automation tools for data integrity checks, and providing ongoing training to employees to maximize the long-term impact of governance on data quality.

2. What are the critical success factors for implementing data governance frameworks in large organizations?

The critical success factors for implementing data governance frameworks in large organizations were identified through quantitative analysis, including factor analysis, regression models, and cluster analysis, as well as stakeholder perceptions gathered from survey responses. The findings highlight several key determinants of governance success, with senior management support, resource availability, training and awareness, role clarity, and inter-departmental communication emerging as the most influential factors.

The factor analysis revealed two distinct but complementary dimensions that drive governance success: internal readiness and collaborative communication. Internal readiness, which includes adequate resource allocation, training programs, and clearly defined roles and responsibilities, serves as the foundation for governance effectiveness. Resource availability had the strongest impact among these factors, emphasizing the need for organizations to invest in governance infrastructure, technology, and skilled personnel. The lack of these foundational elements, as confirmed by regression analysis, was a major barrier to successful governance implementation.

The second dimension, collaborative communication, highlights the importance of cross-functional coordination and stakeholder engagement. The correlation matrix showed a significant positive relationship between inter-departmental communication and governance success ($r = 0.502$), indicating that organizations with strong collaboration between business units and IT teams achieve better governance outcomes. The survey results reinforced this, with 97.3% of respondents agreeing or strongly agreeing that effective communication across departments is essential for governance implementation. This finding underscores that governance frameworks cannot function in isolation but must be integrated into the organization's broader operational and strategic processes.

The cluster analysis provided further insights into governance readiness by categorizing organizations into three groups based on their governance preparedness: highly prepared organizations, moderately prepared organizations, and organizations facing challenges. Highly prepared organizations, which had strong leadership commitment, well-defined governance roles, and robust training programs, were the most successful in implementing governance frameworks. Moderately prepared organizations had a solid governance foundation but needed improvements in training and awareness to elevate their readiness levels. Organizations facing challenges, on the other hand, struggled with governance implementation due to resource constraints, lack of role clarity, and weak cross-departmental collaboration.

Regression analysis results further emphasized the role of senior management support in governance success. Organizations where leadership actively endorsed governance initiatives saw significantly higher adoption rates and effectiveness. 80% of survey respondents strongly agreed that executive buy-in is critical for successful governance implementation. The absence of leadership involvement was a major impediment in organizations that struggled with governance adoption, as decision-makers often deprioritized governance initiatives due to competing business demands.

Additionally, the training and awareness factor emerged as a crucial success driver. The survey results showed that 99.3% of respondents agreed or strongly agreed that training and awareness programs were necessary for governance success. This finding was supported by the Likert scale analysis, which indicated that organizations with well-structured training programs experienced higher compliance rates, improved data handling practices, and reduced governance resistance. The lack of training was a key issue in organizations with lower governance maturity, where employees lacked the necessary skills to implement and maintain governance frameworks effectively.

3. How do stakeholder perceptions influence the adoption and success of data governance frameworks?

Stakeholder perceptions play a pivotal role in the adoption and success of data governance frameworks, as evidenced by the quantitative analysis, descriptive statistics, Likert scale analysis, and correlation tests conducted in this study. The findings suggest that positive stakeholder perceptions significantly enhance governance adoption, while challenges such as resistance to change, resource limitations, and perceived complexity can act as barriers to successful implementation.

The descriptive statistics and Likert scale analysis demonstrated that stakeholders overwhelmingly recognize the benefits of data governance frameworks. The survey results indicated that 92.9% of respondents agreed or strongly agreed that data governance positively impacts organizational efficiency and decision-making. This strong endorsement suggests that when stakeholders perceive governance as beneficial, they are more likely to support and actively engage in governance initiatives, leading to higher adoption rates and more effective implementation.

However, resistance to change emerged as a major challenge in governance adoption. 93.3% of participants acknowledged resistance to change as a significant obstacle, highlighting the difficulty organizations face in shifting from unstructured data management practices to formal governance frameworks. The correlation analysis revealed a strong association between resistance to change and lower governance success rates (r = -0.57), confirming that organizations struggling with change management often face governance implementation failures. This underscores the need for targeted change management strategies, including effective communication, leadership involvement, and employee engagement, to address concerns and foster a culture of data accountability.

The study also found that perceived resource constraints significantly impact governance adoption. The Likert scale analysis showed that 93% of respondents agreed or strongly agreed that a lack of resources or expertise was a barrier to governance success. This finding was reinforced by the cluster analysis, which categorized organizations based on their governance readiness. Organizations in the "facing challenges" cluster exhibited low adoption rates, primarily due to insufficient resources and limited training opportunities. By contrast, highly prepared organizations with adequate resources and leadership support reported higher adoption rates and successful governance outcomes. These results suggest that stakeholders are more likely to embrace governance initiatives when they feel equipped with the necessary skills, tools, and executive backing.

Another key factor influencing stakeholder perceptions was complexity in governance frameworks. The regression analysis demonstrated that perceived complexity negatively impacts adoption rates, as stakeholders in organizations with more intricate governance structures expressed lower confidence in successful implementation. The Likert scale data indicated that 87.8% of respondents viewed complexity as a significant barrier, further emphasizing the need for simplified governance models, clear guidelines, and user-friendly frameworks. This finding highlights the importance of streamlining governance policies and ensuring they are easily understood and applicable across different organizational levels.

Despite these challenges, the study revealed that stakeholders perceive the benefits of governance to outweigh its challenges. The Likert scale analysis showed that 94.5% of respondents agreed or strongly agreed that the long-term advantages of governance frameworks, such as improved data accuracy, better compliance, and enhanced decision-making, justify the effort required for implementation. This suggests that organizations can leverage these positive perceptions to drive stronger governance adoption by emphasizing its long-term value and aligning governance initiatives with business goals.

CHAPTER VI:
SUMMARY, IMPLICATIONS, AND RECOMMENDATIONS

6.1 Summary

This dissertation explores the impact of data governance frameworks on data quality, business outcomes, and decision-making processes in large organizations. With the increasing reliance on data-driven strategies, ensuring data accuracy, security, compliance, and governance effectiveness has become critical for organizations operating in complex environments. This research adopts a quantitative approach to evaluate the measurable benefits of governance frameworks, identify critical success factors, and analyze stakeholder perceptions regarding governance adoption and challenges.

The study confirms that effective data governance frameworks lead to significant improvements in data quality, operational efficiency, and strategic decision-making. Statistical analyses, including regression, correlation, factor, and cluster analyses, demonstrated that business outcomes improvement is the strongest predictor of governance success, reinforcing the importance of aligning governance frameworks with organizational goals and compliance standards. Other key drivers include data management alignment, post-governance quality improvements, and enhanced decision-making capabilities.

The research identified several critical success factors for implementing governance frameworks, including senior management support, resource availability, training and awareness, and inter-departmental communication. Organizations that demonstrated higher readiness in these areas experienced better governance adoption rates and operational efficiencies. The factor analysis revealed two key dimensions—internal readiness (resources, training, and role clarity) and external collaboration (inter-departmental communication and leadership support)—that determine governance success.

Despite the positive impacts, the study also highlighted major challenges to governance implementation. Resistance to change, lack of resources and expertise, and governance complexity emerged as primary barriers to successful adoption. Over 93% of respondents identified resistance to change as a significant issue, emphasizing the need for structured change management strategies. Similarly, 93% cited resource limitations as a challenge, reinforcing the necessity for investment in technology, skilled personnel, and training programs. Furthermore, 87.8% of participants perceived governance frameworks as complex, indicating the need for simplified, scalable, and user-friendly governance models.

Stakeholder perceptions played a crucial role in governance adoption and success. Organizations with strong leadership involvement, clear governance structures, and stakeholder engagement experienced higher adoption rates and better governance effectiveness. While some challenges were recognized, the study found that 94.5% of participants believed that the benefits of governance frameworks outweigh the challenges, affirming the long-term value of structured governance policies.

The dissertation contributes valuable empirical insights into data governance implementation best practices, providing a framework for organizations to refine their governance models and enhance data-driven decision-making. The findings underscore the importance of strategic alignment, leadership support, stakeholder engagement, and continuous governance improvements to maximize governance effectiveness.

6.2 Implications

This dissertation provides significant implications for both academia and industry by offering empirical evidence on the effectiveness of data governance frameworks in large organizations. The findings reinforce the critical role of structured governance models in enhancing data quality, business outcomes, and decision-making processes. As organizations increasingly rely on data for operational efficiency and strategic planning, the research highlights the necessity of adopting robust governance structures to ensure data accuracy, compliance, and security. The insights from this study provide a foundation for organizations to refine their governance practices, optimize data management strategies, and align governance efforts with broader business objectives.

One of the key implications of this research is its emphasis on business outcome-driven governance models. The study demonstrates that business outcomes improvement is the strongest predictor of governance success, suggesting that organizations must align their governance frameworks with tangible business objectives. Companies that prioritize governance strategies aimed at improving operational efficiency, financial performance, and decision-making processes are more likely to experience measurable benefits. This shifts the traditional perspective of governance as a compliance-driven necessity to a value-generating strategic asset, encouraging organizations to integrate governance practices into their long-term business planning.

The research also has important implications for organizational leadership and change management. With resistance to change identified as a major barrier, the findings suggest that senior management support and stakeholder engagement are essential for successful governance implementation. Organizations must invest in change management strategies, including training programs, internal communication efforts, and leadership-driven initiatives, to foster a governance culture. This study highlights the need for leadership-driven governance adoption, where executives actively participate in governance processes to ensure organization-wide commitment and compliance.

Additionally, the dissertation underscores the importance of resource allocation in governance implementation. The lack of resources and expertise emerged as a critical challenge, with over 93% of participants citing resource constraints as a barrier to governance success. This implies that organizations must prioritize investments in data governance technology, workforce training, and infrastructure development. Without sufficient resources, governance initiatives may fail to deliver the intended improvements in data quality and business performance. Therefore, decision-makers should allocate dedicated budgets for governance programs and ensure that the necessary tools and technologies are in place to support governance effectiveness.

From a technological perspective, the findings suggest that simplifying governance frameworks and integrating automation can enhance adoption and efficiency. The study revealed that complexity in governance structures is a major deterrent, with 87.8% of participants agreeing that governance frameworks can be difficult to implement and sustain. Organizations should focus on designing governance models that are scalable, adaptable, and easy to implement, leveraging artificial intelligence, automation, and cloud-based solutions to streamline governance processes. By simplifying data governance policies and using automation tools to enforce compliance, organizations can reduce complexity and increase adoption rates.

Furthermore, this research has significant policy implications for regulatory bodies and compliance frameworks. With increasing global emphasis on data privacy regulations such as GDPR and HIPAA, organizations need structured governance policies to ensure compliance and mitigate legal risks. The study's findings support the development of standardized governance models that align with regulatory requirements while also being adaptable to industry-specific needs. Policymakers and industry regulators can use these insights to design flexible yet robust governance guidelines that promote data integrity, transparency, and accountability across various sectors.

Lastly, this dissertation contributes to academic research by bridging the gap between theoretical governance models and practical implementation challenges. The study validates existing governance theories while providing empirical evidence on their effectiveness in real-world organizational contexts. Future research can build upon these findings by exploring longitudinal governance impacts, sector-specific governance challenges, and emerging governance technologies such as blockchain and AI-driven governance automation.

6.3 Recommendations for Future Research

This dissertation has provided significant insights into the impact of data governance frameworks on data quality, business outcomes, and decision-making processes in large organizations. However, there are several areas where future research can further expand upon the findings and address existing gaps in the field.

One of the primary recommendations for future research is to conduct longitudinal studies to assess the long-term impact of data governance frameworks. This study used a cross-sectional approach, which provides a snapshot of the current governance landscape. However, governance effectiveness evolves over time, influenced by changing regulatory requirements, technological advancements, and organizational shifts. Future studies should adopt longitudinal research methodologies to track the effectiveness of governance frameworks over extended periods, measuring how governance strategies adapt to new challenges and opportunities.

Another key area for future exploration is the sector-specific analysis of governance challenges and success factors. While this research included participants from multiple industries, it identified variations in governance adoption across sectors, with finance and healthcare demonstrating higher implementation levels compared to manufacturing and retail. Future studies should examine industry-specific governance models, focusing on how different regulatory environments, technological infrastructure, and organizational priorities impact governance effectiveness. Conducting comparative studies across industries can provide deeper insights into the unique challenges and best practices within specific domains.

Additionally, future research should explore the role of emerging technologies in data governance automation. The findings highlighted that complexity in governance implementation is a major barrier, with 87.8% of participants acknowledging the challenge of managing intricate governance structures. As artificial intelligence (AI), machine learning, and blockchain continue to evolve, future research should investigate how these technologies can streamline governance processes, enhance compliance monitoring, and improve data quality. Examining the adoption of AI-driven governance models and their impact on governance efficiency will be crucial in shaping the future of enterprise data management.

Further research is also needed to explore the human and cultural dimensions of data governance adoption. The study found that resistance to change is one of the most significant barriers to governance success, indicating that organizations struggle with employee buy-in, cultural alignment, and leadership commitment. Future research could examine behavioral and organizational psychology perspectives on governance adoption, identifying strategies for improving governance-related training, change management initiatives, and stakeholder engagement practices. Investigating how organizational culture influences governance success will be essential in developing more effective implementation strategies.

In addition, exploring governance frameworks in small and medium-sized enterprises (SMEs) presents another important avenue for research. This study focused on large organizations, where structured governance models are more prevalent due to regulatory and operational demands. However, SMEs face unique governance challenges, such as limited resources, lack of expertise, and scalability constraints. Future research should explore how governance frameworks can be adapted to smaller organizations, ensuring that governance best practices are accessible and applicable to businesses of all sizes.

Finally, future research should consider the global perspective on data governance, analyzing governance frameworks across different regulatory, economic, and cultural contexts. As data governance becomes a global priority, organizations must navigate varying legal requirements, compliance obligations, and international data-sharing policies. Comparative studies on governance models in different countries and regions can provide valuable insights into how governance strategies can be standardized while remaining adaptable to local regulations and business environments.

6.4 Conclusion

This dissertation has explored the measurable impact of data governance frameworks on data quality, business outcomes, and decision-making processes in large organizations. Through a rigorous quantitative analysis, the study has demonstrated that well-implemented governance frameworks lead to significant improvements in data accuracy, consistency, compliance, and strategic alignment. The findings emphasize that effective data governance is not merely a regulatory requirement but a critical enabler of business success, ensuring that organizations can leverage data as a valuable asset for operational efficiency and competitive advantage.

The study confirmed that business outcomes improvement and strategic alignment are the most influential factors driving the success of governance frameworks. Organizations that prioritize governance strategies aligned with business goals experience higher efficiency in decision-making, improved data management processes, and better regulatory compliance. The research also highlighted that the finance and healthcare sectors exhibit the highest levels of governance adoption, while manufacturing and retail face relatively lower engagement, underscoring the need for industry-specific governance strategies.

Additionally, the study identified critical success factors for implementing governance frameworks, including senior management support, role clarity, resource availability, interdepartmental collaboration, and ongoing training initiatives. The results showed that organizations with strong leadership commitment and structured governance models achieve higher governance maturity, improved stakeholder buy-in, and enhanced data-driven decision-making. However, challenges such as resistance to change, lack of expertise, and the complexity of governance implementation remain significant barriers. Addressing these obstacles requires comprehensive change management strategies, investment in governance technology, and fostering a data-centric organizational culture.

Stakeholder perceptions emerged as a crucial determinant of governance success. The study found that most participants recognize the benefits of governance frameworks, but resistance to change and concerns over complexity hinder adoption. This highlights the need for organizations to focus on improving stakeholder engagement, increasing governance awareness, and simplifying governance structures to enhance adoption rates and long-term sustainability.

The research also provided empirical validation for the interconnected nature of governance elements, demonstrating that improvements in one governance dimension drive progress in others. The strong correlations between business outcomes, data quality, decision-making efficiency, and process optimization reinforce the necessity of a holistic and integrated approach to governance implementation. Organizations that align governance strategies with business objectives and continuously refine governance models achieve superior performance, better risk management, and long-term sustainability.

While this study has contributed valuable insights into the field of enterprise data governance, it also highlights areas for future research. There is a need for longitudinal studies to assess governance impact over time, industry-specific analyses to tailor governance models to different sectors, and further exploration of emerging technologies like AI and blockchain in automating governance processes. Additionally, expanding research on the cultural and behavioral aspects of governance adoption can provide deeper insights into overcoming organizational resistance and enhancing governance effectiveness.

APPENDIX A
QUSTIONNAIRE

Demographic Details

1. **Age:**
   - 18-25
   - 26-35
   - 36-45
   - 46-55
   - 56 and above
2. **Gender:**
   - Male
   - Female
   - Non-binary
   - Prefer not to say
3. **Position in the organisation :**
   - Entry-Level
   - Mid-Level Management
   - Senior Management
   - Executive
4. **Industry Sector:**
   - Finance
   - Healthcare
   - Technology
   - Manufacturing
   - Retail
   - Other (Please specify)
5. **Years of Experience in the Industry:**
   - 0-5 years
   - 6-10 years
   - 11-15 years
   - 16-20 years
   - 21 years and above

Section 1: Relationship Between Data Governance Frameworks and Business Outcomes

1. The implementation of data governance frameworks has significantly improved the quality of data in our organisation .
   - Strongly Disagree
   - Disagree
   - Neutral
   - Agree
   - Strongly Agree
2. Data governance initiatives have led to measurable improvements in our organisation 's strategic business outcomes.
   - Strongly Disagree
   - Disagree
   - Neutral
   - Agree
   - Strongly Agree
3. Our organisation 's data governance framework is directly linked to enhanced decision-making processes.
   - Strongly Disagree
   - Disagree
   - Neutral
   - Agree
   - Strongly Agree
4. The quality of data in our organisation has noticeably improved since the implementation of data governance frameworks.
   - Strongly Disagree
   - Disagree
   - Neutral
   - Agree
   - Strongly Agree
5. Data governance has played a critical role in aligning data management practices with business strategy.
   - Strongly Disagree
   - Disagree
   - Neutral
   - Agree
   - Strongly Agree

Section 2: Critical Factors for Successful Implementation of Data Governance Frameworks

1. Senior management support is crucial for the successful implementation of data governance frameworks.
   - Strongly Disagree
   - Disagree
   - Neutral
   - Agree
   - Strongly Agree
2. Clearly defined roles and responsibilities contribute to the effective implementation of data governance in our organisation .
   - Strongly Disagree
   - Disagree
   - Neutral
   - Agree
   - Strongly Agree
3. Adequate training and awareness programs are essential for the successful adoption of data governance frameworks.
   - Strongly Disagree
   - Disagree
   - Neutral
   - Agree
   - Strongly Agree
4. The availability of necessary resources (e.g., technology, tools, personnel) is critical to the success of data governance initiatives.
   - Strongly Disagree
   - Disagree
   - Neutral
   - Agree
   - Strongly Agree
5. Effective communication between departments is a key factor in the successful implementation of data governance frameworks.
   - Strongly Disagree
   - Disagree
   - Neutral
   - Agree
   - Strongly Agree

Section 3: Stakeholder Perceptions on Benefits, Challenges, and Barriers

1. Stakeholders perceive data governance as beneficial for improving data quality and integrity.
   - Strongly Disagree
   - Disagree
   - Neutral
   - Agree
   - Strongly Agree
2. The adoption of data governance frameworks has been challenging due to resistance to change within the organisation .
   - Strongly Disagree
   - Disagree
   - Neutral
   - Agree
   - Strongly Agree
3. There are significant barriers to the implementation of data governance, such as lack of resources or expertise.
   - Strongly Disagree
   - Disagree
   - Neutral
   - Agree
   - Strongly Agree
4. Stakeholders believe that the benefits of data governance outweigh the challenges encountered during implementation.
   - Strongly Disagree
   - Disagree
   - Neutral
   - Agree
   - Strongly Agree
5. The complexity of data governance frameworks is a barrier to their successful adoption in our organisation .
   - Strongly Disagree
   - Disagree
   - Neutral
   - Agree
   - Strongly Agree

APPENDIX B
INFORMED CONSENT

Research Title: enterprise data management, design of a conceptual model for effective data governance framework in large orginanzations

Principal Investigator: My name is Chadwick Thompson Okoye. I am a DBA learner at SSBM GENEVA. I am conducting a study and you are invited to participate.

Purpose of the Study:

This study seeks to analyze the effectiveness of data governance frameworks and their role in improving data quality, business efficiency, and strategic decision-making. The research aims to identify challenges in governance implementation and provide insights into best practices for large organizations.

Procedures:
If you agree to participate, you will be asked to complete a structured survey. The survey will include questions about your experiences, preferences, and perceptions regarding health insurance marketing strategies. It will take approximately 15–20 minutes to complete.

Confidentiality:
All information you provide will be kept confidential and used solely for academic purposes. Your responses will be anonymized to ensure that no personally identifiable information is included in the study's results. The data will be securely stored and accessed only by the researcher and authorized personnel.

Potential Risks and Benefits:

There are no significant risks associated with participating in this study. Your participation will contribute to valuable insights into improving health insurance marketing strategies, which may ultimately benefit consumers and the industry.

REFERENCES

Achanta, M., Data Governance in the Age of Cloud Computing: Strategies and Considerations.

Achanta, R. (2023) 'Impact of Cloud Computing on Enterprise Data Management and Governance', *Journal of Cloud Computing & Data Governance*, 19(1), pp. 45-61.

Adebayo, K., Singh, P. and Zhao, H. (2024) 'Data Governance for Regulatory Compliance and Risk Mitigation', *Enterprise Risk Management Journal*, 21(1), pp. 45-62.

Aguboshim, C., Patel, J. and Osei, A. (2023) 'The DAMA International Guide to Data Governance: A Conceptual Framework for Information Security', *Journal of Data Security and Governance*, 12(2), pp. 49-63.

Akokodaripon, D., Alonge-Essiet, F. O., Aderoju, A. V., & Reis, O. (2024). *Implementing Data Governance in Financial Systems: Strategies for Ensuring Compliance and Security in Multi-Source Data Integration Projects*. Computer Science & IT Research Journal.

Al-Badi, A., Tarhini, A. and Khan, A.I., 2018. Exploring big data governance frameworks. *Procedia computer science*, *141*, pp.271-277.

Algarni, A., Al-Mohammad, K. and Hassan, S. (2021) 'Quantitative Assessment Models for Cyber Risk Mitigation in Data Governance', *Cybersecurity and Risk Management Review*, 8(4), pp. 103-118.

Al-Rashid, W., Alshawi, M. and Al-Mashari, M., 2013, July. ERP Implementation Success through Effective Management of Roles and Responsibilities among StakeholdersA Holistic Framework Adopted from Two Case Studies. In *Third International Symposium on Business Modeling and Software Design* (Vol. 1, pp. 157-165). SCITEPRESS.

Al-Sai, M., Jasim, H. and Ahmed, Z. (2020) 'A Comprehensive Framework for Data Governance: Integrating Organizational, Technological, and

Analytical Aspects', *Enterprise Information Systems Journal*, 11(3), pp. 77-95.

Alshamsi, M., Tariq, Z. and Khan, F. (2020) 'The Role of AI and Blockchain in Enhancing Governance Transparency: A Conceptual Modeling Approach', *Journal of Emerging Technologies in Governance*, 6(1), pp. 45-59.

Ashraf, M. (2023) 'Scalable Data Architectures: Data Lakes and Warehouses in Enterprise Platforms', *Big Data & Information Systems Review*, 9(3), pp. 150-172.

Babu, M.S., Raj, K.B. and Devi, D.A., 2021. Data security and sensitive data protection using privacy by design technique. In *2nd EAI International Conference on Big Data Innovation for Sustainable Cognitive Computing: BDCC 2019* (pp. 177-189). Springer International Publishing.

Bassi, C. and Alves-Souza, S. (2023) 'Enterprise Data Management Challenges Across Market Segments', *Global Business Review*, 18(3), pp. 67-85.

Bassi, C., Alves-Souza, S. and Gomes, P. (2024) 'Enhancing Organizational Performance with Data Governance Programs', *Journal of Data Strategy and Governance*, 20(1), pp. 102-118.

Bento, F., Costa, C. and Pereira, R. (2022) 'The Role of Data Governance in Standardization and Accessibility of Organizational Data', *International Journal of Information Management*, 13(2), pp. 101-119.

Bhatia, P. and Kumar, R. (2020) *Data Governance Strategies: Ensuring Data Integrity and Compliance*. London: Springer.

Biagi, R. and Russo, F. (2022) 'Data Models for IT Governance Implementation: Overcoming Challenges in Data Utilization', *International Journal of Information Systems and Governance*, 13(2), pp. 95-112.

Black, L., Johnson, P. and Scott, M. (2023) 'Enhancing Organizational Competitiveness through Data Governance', *Journal of Business and Information Management*, 15(2), pp. 54-70.

Burton, P. (2021) 'Shaping a Data-Driven Culture through Effective Data Governance', *Journal of Organizational Data Management*, 18(3), pp. 47-64.

Chakravorty, R. (2020) *Data Governance and Leadership Challenges: A Comprehensive Approach*. New York: Wiley.

Chandra, R., Patel, S. and Gupta, M. (2023) 'Critical Success Factors for Data Governance in Data-Driven Decision Making', *Journal of Data Management and Governance*, 14(1), pp. 55-72.

Chukwurah, N., Adeyemi, O. and Patel, R. (2024) 'Effective Data Governance Frameworks: Policies, Roles, and Standards', *Journal of Data Governance and Management*, 16(1), pp. 34-52.

Chukwurah, N., Ige, A.B., Idemudia, C. and Adebayo, V.I., 2024. Strategies for engaging stakeholders in data governance: Building effective communication and collaboration. *Open Access Research Journal of Multidisciplinary Studies*, *8*(01), pp.057-067.

Coche, J., Fernández, L. and Russo, M. (2023) 'Navigating Cross-Border Data Governance: Regulatory Challenges and Compliance Strategies', *International Journal of Data Privacy & Security*, 18(2), pp. 67-85.

Davenport, T. H., & Bean, R. (2018). *Data-Driven Organizations: Realizing the Potential of AI and Analytics*. MIT Sloan Management Review, **59**(3), 15-20.

Dehghani, Z. (2022). *Data Mesh: Delivering Data-Driven Value at Scale*. O'Reilly Media, **1**(1), 50-60.

Desani, S. (2023) 'AI-Driven Data Quality Management and Automation for Enhanced Data Integrity and Compliance', *Journal of Data Governance and Automation*, 12(1), pp. 88-105.

Dingre, S. (2023). *Exploration of Data Governance Frameworks, Roles, and Metrics for Success*. Journal of Artificial Intelligence & Cloud Computing.

Dreibelbis, A. (2020). *Enterprise Data Governance: Managing Data as an Organizational Asset*. McGraw-Hill, **4**(2), 30-45.

Efunniyi, C. P., Abhulimen, A. O., Obiki-Osafiele, A. N., Osundare, O. S., Agu, E. E., & Adeniran, I. A. (2024). *Strengthening Corporate Governance and Financial Compliance: Enhancing Accountability and Transparency*. Finance & Accounting Research Journal.

Endutkin, V. (2020) 'Automating Corporate Governance Procedures for Improved Performance and Management Effectiveness', *International Journal of Business and Governance*, 9(2), pp. 45-59.

Fattah, S. (2024) *Building a Data-Driven Culture with Effective Data Governance Policies*. London: Routledge.

Gartner. (2023). *The Future of Enterprise Data Management: Trends and Predictions*. Gartner Research.

Gartner. (2023). *Top Trends in Data and Analytics for 2023*. Gartner Research, **5**(1), 5-15.

Hartley, N., Kunz, W. and Tarbit, J., 2024. The corporate digital responsibility (CDR) calculus: How and why organizations reconcile digital and ethical trade-offs for growth. *Organizational Dynamics*, *53*(2), p.101056.

Hashem, I. A. T., et al. (2015). The Role of Cloud Computing in Big Data Management. *Journal of Cloud Computing, 4*(1), 1-16.

Herschel, R. (2021) *Business Intelligence and Data Management: Strategies for Success*. New York: Routledge.

Huff, R. and Lee, J. (2020) 'Data as a Strategic Asset: Governance for Better Decision Making and Risk Management', *Strategic Data Management Review*, 8(3), pp. 112-130.

Inmon, W. H. (1992). *Building the Data Warehouse*. John Wiley & Sons.

Islam, A., 2024. DATA GOVERNANCE AND COMPLIANCE IN CLOUD-BASED BIG DATA ANALYTICS: A DATABASE-CENTRIC REVIEW.

Islam, R. (2024) 'AI, Machine Learning, and Blockchain in Cloud-Based Big Data Analytics for Governance', *Journal of Artificial Intelligence and Data Compliance*, 15(1), pp. 23-41.

Islam, R. (2024) 'Real-Time Monitoring and Predictive Compliance Risk Assessment in Data Governance', *Journal of Artificial Intelligence and Data Compliance*, 15(1), pp. 23-41.

Jagadish, H. V. (2015). Big Data and Its Technological Challenges. *Communications of the ACM, 58*(7), 86-94.

Jagals, M., 2021. Expanding data governance across company boundaries–an inter-organizational perspective of roles and responsibilities. In *The Practice of Enterprise Modeling: 14th IFIP WG 8.1 Working Conference, PoEM 2021, Riga, Latvia, November 24–26, 2021, Proceedings 14* (pp. 245-254). Springer International Publishing.

Jiang, L. and Li, X. (2024) 'Blockchain and Decentralized Governance: The Role of Smart Contracts and DAOs', *Journal of Digital Governance and Innovation*, 11(2), pp. 134-148.

Kaddoumi, A. and Tambo, T. (2023) 'The Role of Chief Data Officers and Enterprise Architects in Achieving Enterprise Data Agility', *Journal of Enterprise Architecture and Data Management*, 12(1), pp. 88-104.

Karkosková, M. (2022) 'A Data Governance Model Based on BCBS 239 and DAMA Methodology for Financial Institutions', *International Journal of Financial Data Management*, 13(2), pp. 56-72.

Khatri, V., & Brown, C. V. (2010). Designing Data Governance. *Communications of the ACM, 53*(1), 148-152.

Kimball, R., & Ross, M. (2013). *The Data Warehouse Toolkit: The Definitive Guide to Dimensional Modeling*. John Wiley & Sons.

Knosp, L., Adams, J. and Ransom, B. (2022) 'Challenges in Developing and Maintaining Enterprise Data Warehouses for Research: A Cloud Migration Perspective', *Journal of Clinical Data Systems*, 8(4), pp. 34-49.

Koilakonda, A. (2024) *Effective Data Governance for Business Value and Competitive Advantage*. London: Springer.

Kumar, R., Sharma, P. and Gupta, M. (2024) 'Data Governance Frameworks for Enhancing Cybersecurity and Preventing Data Breaches', *Journal of Information Security and Governance*, 14(1), pp. 62-78.

Leghemo, I.M., Azubuike, C., Segun-Falade, O.D. and Odionu, C.S., 2025. Data governance for emerging technologies: A conceptual framework for managing blockchain, IoT, and AI. *Journal of Engineering Research and Reports*, *27*(1), pp.247-267.

Liu, X. (2022) 'Data Security in Cloud-Based Governance: A Comprehensive Approach', *International Journal of Information Security Management*, 14(3), pp. 98-112.

Locke, P. and Bird, S. (2020) 'AI and Automation in Corporate Governance: Enhancing Risk Assessment and Compliance', *Journal of Corporate Governance and Technology*, 22(3), pp. 100-115.

Madhavan, D. (2024). *Enterprise Data Governance: A Comprehensive Framework for Ensuring Data Integrity, Security, and Compliance in Modern Organizations*. International Journal of Scientific Research in Computer Science, Engineering and Information Technology.

Madhavan, R. (2024) *Enterprise Data Governance: Maximizing Data Value and Ensuring Compliance*. New York: Routledge.

Mahardika, F. and Sumantri, R. (2020) 'Enterprise Data Management Architecture for Distributed Campuses', *International Journal of Enterprise Information Systems*, 16(2), pp. 45-60.

Manigonda, V. (2023) 'Automated Processes and Centralized Dashboards for Data Governance Transparency', *International Journal of Automation and Data Governance*, 7(2), pp. 56-72.

Martijn, N., Hulstijn, J., Bruijne, M., & Tan, Y. H. (2015). *Determining the Effects of Data Governance on the Performance and Compliance of Enterprises in the Logistics and Retail Sector*.

Matai, P. (2022). *Beyond Compliance: Balancing Risk and Innovation with Effective Data Governance in Financial Services*. International Journal of Science and Research.

Mathrani, A. (2021) 'Context-Specific Data Transformation in Business Intelligence', *International Journal of Business Analytics*, 12(3), pp. 78-95.

MERKUS, J., HELMS, R.W. and KUSTERS, R., 2023. DATA GOVERNANCE CAPABILITIES; EMPIRICAL VALIDATION IN CASE STUDIES OF LARGE ORGANISATIONS. *36th Bled eConference Digital Economy and*

Society: The Balancing Act for Digital Innovation in Times of Instability, p.35.

Micheli, M., Anderson, K. and Liu, X. (2020) 'Emerging Trends in Data Governance: Data Sharing Pools, Cooperatives, and Public Trusts', *Journal of Data Governance and Public Policy*, 17(2), pp. 45-60.

Miloslavskaya, N., & Tolstoy, A. (2019). Data Lifecycle Management in the Digital Economy. *Future Generation Computer Systems,* 94, 160-172.

Nambiar, A.M. and Mundra, D. (2022) 'Big Data Management Challenges: Issues of Quality, Ownership, and Access', *International Journal of Data Science and Analytics*, 10(4), pp. 112-128.

Negro, J. and Mesia, L. (2020) *Business Intelligence: Data Collection and Decision Making in Organizations*. London: Springer.

Neupane, M. (2023) 'Digital Governance Frameworks: AI and Automation in Public Service Delivery', *Journal of Public Administration and Technology*, 18(1), pp. 78-92.

Niu, Y., Zhang, H. and Li, X. (2021) 'Optimized Data Management using Big Data Analytics: A Framework for Enhancing Organizational Effectiveness', *Journal of Big Data Management*, 8(2), pp. 45-67.

Pansara, M. (2021) 'Best Practices for Data Governance in Cloud-Based Environments', *Cloud Computing & Information Security Review*, 13(1), pp. 77-94.

Rajaretnam, M. (2020) *Managing Cybersecurity Risks through Effective Data Governance*. New York: Wiley.

Rakshith, V. and Pawar, A. (2024) 'Cloud-Based Data Governance: Ensuring Compliance and Business Continuity', *Cloud Computing & Information Security Review*, 13(1), pp. 77-94.

Redman, T. C. (2016). *Data Driven: Profiting from Your Most Important Business Asset*. Harvard Business Review Press, **12**(3), 74-80.

Riandi, R., Subekti, I. and Purwanto, A. (2021) 'A Conceptual Model for Measuring E-Learning System Success Using User Satisfaction as a

Mediator', *International Journal of Educational Technology*, 9(3), pp. 98-113.

Sandhu, M. (2021) 'The Integration of Big Data with Cloud Computing: Opportunities, Challenges, and Future Directions', *Big Data Research Journal*, 11(2), pp. 102-118.

Schmuck, L. and Georgescu, S. (2024) 'Adapting the DeLone and McLean Information Systems Success Measurement Model for Data Governance Effectiveness', *Journal of Data Governance and Information Systems*, 19(1), pp. 23-40.

Seneviratne, O., et al. (2022). AI and Cybersecurity in Data Management. *Journal of Data Science & Security*, **12**(3), 210-217.

Seneviratne, O., et al. (2022). AI-Driven Data Governance in Modern Enterprises. *Journal of Data Science & Analytics, 10*(4), 211-229.

Sharma, P., Verma, R. and Gupta, S. (2022) 'Legal and Ethical Challenges in Data Governance: Implications for Organizations', *Journal of Business Ethics and Compliance*, 15(3), pp. 112-129.

Shinta Oktaviana, R., Wijaya, H. and Adinugroho, D. (2024) 'Policy Challenges in Enterprise Data Management: A Case Study in Healthcare', *Journal of Information Systems Management*, 15(1), pp. 22-38.

Styrin, E. (2023) 'The Impact of AI and Blockchain on Data Governance: Security and Cultural Barriers', *International Journal of Digital Governance*, 12(2), pp. 89-105.

Wu, T., 2024. Exploring of the Integration of Emerging Technologies and Corporate Governance. *Advances in Economics, Management and Political Sciences*, *87*, pp.90-96.

Yallop, D. and Séraphin, T. (2020) 'Ethical, Privacy, and Security Concerns in Big Data Governance', *Journal of Information Security and Ethics*, 10(3), pp. 150-167

Zeng, M., et al. (2021). The Importance of Metadata Management for Enterprise AI. *Information Systems Journal, 32*(2), 312-335.

www.ingramcontent.com/pod-product-compliance
Ingram Content Group UK Ltd.
Pitfield, Milton Keynes, MK11 3LW, UK
UKHW021830270726
14058UKWH00001B/70

9 798892 489492